The Star Treatment

The Star Treatment

by Dick Stelzer

The Bobbs-Merrill Company, Inc.
Indianapolis/New York

Published by The Bobbs-Merrill Company, Inc.
Indianapolis New York

Designed by Holly McNeely
Manufactured in the United States of America

First printing

Library of Congress Cataloging in Publication Data

Stelzer, Dick.
The star treatment

1. Entertainers—United States—Biography.
2. Authors, American—20th century—Biography.
3. Psychotherapy—Cases, clinical reports, statistics.
I. Title.

PN2285.S719 791.43'0922
[B] 77-76868
ISBN 0-672-52290-X

To my Producers
in Nashville

Table of Contents

The Star Treatment

Introduction

This is a book about psychotherapy, based on interviews with a fascinating group of people who told me about their experiences with psychologists, psychiatrists and analysts—and the problems that led them to see these professionals.

It is also, as it turns out, an undeniably positive look at therapy. For the most part, the people in this book have had successful involvements with psychotherapy—or at least have come away from the experience with the belief that they have been helped. This fact may help account for their willingness to acknowledge and discuss their therapy.

Although a playwright, a director, a lyricist, a critic and two writers are among those interviewed in this book, the majority of the subjects are performers. It occurred to me that well-known persons in other fields—such as sports, politics and business—might be logical subjects, but I was unable to find anyone who would talk. People in these occupations were loath even to admit having had any experience with therapy, much less discuss it.

With some self-consciousness, I wrote Pentagon Papers figure Daniel Ellsberg to ask if I might interview him for the book. Why I thought he would want to give away information which top government officials had attempted to obtain through burglarizing his psychiatrist's office is perhaps beyond rational explanation (although equally improbable scenarios have occurred). With no slight sense of irony, he turned me down. "I know your intentions are respectable," he wrote, "but I don't believe in invading my own privacy—or in doing various plumbers' work for them."

Industrialist–art patron Norton Simon agreed to meet with me, but when we sat down at his Malibu house, *he* asked all the questions. Simon was interested in knowing all about the thinking behind the book, the tack I was taking, my own background and familiarity with the subject, and many other details. (When I mentioned the name of my publisher, he noted casually that he believed he had almost bought the company at one time.) Many of his questions had a philosophical slant. Seeing his brilliant and probing mind at work firsthand was fascinating, although I must confess it was uncomfortable having the tables turned on me so unexpectedly by such a master interrogator. (Simon's involvement with therapy, incidentally, began indirectly and on a corporate level. Thanks to his vision, his company was in the vanguard in recognizing the wisdom of making therapy available to the upper echelons of management.)

Because of the subject of my book, I received almost no cooperation from press agents, who normally serve as the liaisons between celebrities and the press. Apparently the word "therapy" is a genuine bugaboo among many of the Hollywood PR people charged with developing and disseminating the public images of their clients. Many of these people obviously view psychotherapy as something sinister—if not akin to voodoo—and a topic of conversation from which their clients should be steered away. So, with amazing omnipotence, most immediately denied—without even checking—that the people they represented had ever gone through any type of therapy; others just said their people would not want to discuss such matters.

It quickly became obvious to me that it would be necessary to contact each potential interviewee directly, circumventing the channels one normally follows to reach public figures.

This was a difficult and time-consuming task. In some cases, I literally spent months in pursuit of a given interviewee, coping with—among other things—schedules that took the person out of town or left him or her with no free time.

In the course of my work on this project, I approached nearly two hundred persons directly or indirectly about the book. In some instances I had advance word—usually reliable—that the individual in question had been in treatment and was at least eligible for inclusion in the book. In other cases, I had no firm knowledge of whether or not the potential interviewee had actually been in therapy. (Once I was asked rather sharply, "Who told you I was in analysis?" to which I had to reply, quite honestly, "No one.")

Some people were uptight at even the suggestion that they might have been in therapy; others were matter-of-fact about their involvement in it (though some of these chose not to see me). "That's something I really don't want to share with anyone" was a response I heard more than once. "No" with no explanation—or no response at all—was all that was forthcoming from others. ("I've never even shaken hands with a psychiatrist" was novelist Irwin Shaw's emphatic reply to my inquiry.)

Several actors, including Peter Strauss (of *Rich Man, Poor Man* fame), told me they had not been in therapy but suggested that perhaps I should check back with them again in a few years.

Director Billy Wilder commented wryly that, although he was born in Freud's native Vienna, he knew nothing about psychoanalysis or any other type of therapy.

Poolside in Beverly Hills, Tennessee Williams said, "I want to leave all that behind me now," when asked to discuss his experiences in analysis.

Science-fiction writer Ray Bradbury indicated he had not been in therapy but volunteered some provocative thoughts: "For what it's worth, being in love and doing what you love cures everything. For me, anyway. Others? I have no answers. . . . All I can offer as a solution is work and love, love and work."

One famous director spoke with me, only to decide a short time later that he was embarrassed about what he had told me and wanted to withdraw his interview. "My thoughts are much too confusing," he wrote, "almost dangerously so, and I believe that if some of the things I said were to appear in print, they might damage or at least upset some people. It is obvious to me that I do not have a clear-cut feeling about analysis and should not even make an attempt to discuss it."

About midway through one interview, I discovered that several minutes of conversation had been lost because I had unknowingly run out of tape. When a new cassette was installed, the person with whom I was speaking amazed me by being able to repeat almost verbatim—as if from a script—that portion of her story which had not been recorded.

Some of the interviews took on certain aspects of actual therapy sessions, although this phenomenon was certainly not intended and came as a surprise at first. One actor actually phoned me the morning after we spoke to say that he realized after I had left his house that during our interview I had somehow become the doctor and he the patient.

Most of the people with whom I met were able to open up and speak freely almost immediately. Others were somewhat guarded in the beginning, although fortunately whatever barriers were up seemed to tumble after we chatted for a short while. In the end, I felt that almost everyone had communicated with unusual candor and had touched on areas that were highly personal, sensitive, and sometimes painful. What they told me was sometimes funny, often touching, and always revealing.

Some readers, no doubt, will identify with certain problems and predicaments discussed in these pages. And this, perhaps, will enable them to better understand or handle their own.

And for readers whose own problems sometimes seem overwhelming, or impossible to cope with, or just unpleasant, maybe the notion of seeking some type of professional help will appear more logical and less threatening. As the testimony of the accomplished people in this book clearly suggests, there are few among us who could not benefit from a greater knowledge of ourselves and the forces at work within us.

Mel Brooks

Mel Brooks is a writer and director whose films include *The Producers, Blazing Saddles, Young Frankenstein* and *Silent Movie.* Brooks worked as a comedy writer for Sid Caesar before he first gained recognition as "The 2000-Year-Old Man." He is married to actress Anne Bancroft.

I was involved in analysis between the ages of twenty-two and twenty-seven. I think it did me good, because I was vomiting between parked cars for a long time before analysis.

One of the great things about psychoanalysis is that it teaches you that physical symptoms are sometimes a mask we hide behind. So, rather than dealing with the real thing—which has to do with the ability to function—we retreat into symptoms. I thought these symptoms were the beginning and the end. Psychoanalysis, thank God, taught me they *were* just symptoms and not the end of my life.

My therapist was a strict Freudian: You weren't allowed to smoke on the couch. You *were* allowed to talk about everything except dreams about your mother; if you did that, he'd slap you. His name was Dr. Clement Staff. He was a wonderful guy and a marvelous analyst.

He really saved me from a lot of despair and unhappiness. One of the biggest things you learn is that through diligent effort combating depressions and applying some positive psychoanalytic techniques, you not only can keep some kind of mental equilibrium but also can reach a kind of joy in living.

It frees you from so much bullshit that keeps you from really defining what is troubling you. What it did for me was clear up many blocks and help me function much more positively. It in no way took away any special neurotic code that allowed for creativity.

After two and a half or three years of therapy, I realized that I couldn't have functioned or survived without it. It's helped me later in my life with my writing, because I'm less inhibited and more in touch with unconscious realities. Psychoanalysis teaches you to get in touch with subliminal thinking, which is very important for a writer. If it did nothing but crush my societally taught sense of shame—do you understand what I'm saying?—that was enough; that was plenty to free me.

Sometimes I get a little criticism from people vis-à-vis taste, and I think if they were psychoanalyzed, that criticism would vaporize. A lot of people don't know the difference between satirizing bad taste and bad taste itself.

One of the things against therapy is that it's very costly. Unless you really need it, sometimes if you talk to a smart neighbor you can save a lot of money.

Richard Benjamin

A middle-aged woman had had a flat tire outside of Richard Benjamin's two-story brick house in Beverly Hills, and he courteously invited her in and showed her to his phone. His concern over her predicament and interest in being a considerate host until help arrived was persistent. In fact, twice during our interview he halted mid-sentence to make sure the woman's problem was being handled.

His young son's toys and beach ball (with "Baskin-Robbins 31 Flavors" embossed on it) and a photograph of his wife, Paula Prentiss, were reminders of the two other members of the Benjamin household, neither of whom was present this sunny morning.

The star of *Goodbye, Columbus, The Diary of a Mad Housewife, The Sunshine Boys* and the old *He & She* TV series wore a denim shirt, blue jeans and black loafers. He conversed in a soft and deliberate manner, sometimes chuckling quietly at the thought of his behavior at certain points prior to and during his time in analysis.

I decided to go into analysis because my wife, Paula Prentiss, was in therapy, and I could see immediately that it was something extraordinary for her. And also I saw that while I thought I was all right, there were things bothering me. But I didn't know what those things were; I just thought that was the way life was.

Before going into therapy, Paula had had a nervous breakdown. She was in this nuthouse, the Payne-Whitney clinic, for seven or eight months. We didn't know it at the time, but she should only have been there—if at all—for two weeks.

I thought the problem was just Paula's. I didn't know I helped put her there. This is the way I saw the problem: I had this very talented, beautiful wife who was just sick. That was all there was to it. We didn't know anything about anything. We were like these two animals, you know. We didn't know what was happening. We just thought this was life.

When Paula went into therapy, I was amazed at the way it helped her. I figured I'd better go into analysis, too, or otherwise I'm going to be left behind in the dust.

I started going to see the same analyst as Paula, a woman named Mildred Newman. Other people who were in analysis would always look at us in a very strange way and say, "My God, you're going to the same analyst? That's not possible, is it?"

But actually it was. Mildred is so extraordinary that I don't believe she talks to any two people the same way. She told me the other day that there are no categories; there's just each person. So there wasn't any kind of conflict.

When I tried to compare notes, Paula wouldn't put up with it. She's too smart. I might say, "Did you tell Mildred about so and so?" and she'd say, "That's none of your business." So I didn't get too far.

I felt comfortable with Mildred personally because she's extraordinary. But I was so uncomfortable in the situation [analysis] that I resisted it and told her that what she was saying was a lot of crap.

I just wanted her to tell me what was wrong with me. I

didn't realize that it's a deep process that takes time. After a while you really understand the meaningful line at the end of *Portnoy's Complaint* when he says, "Now we can begin." It's interesting because it's the truth: you gotta go through a lot of bad jokes before you can start.

In the beginning I was sort of defensive. There was a couch in the office, and I said, "You'll never see me on that couch, because I'm not sick." You think the couch means you're crazy, whereas using the chair means you're just talking to a person in an office. Finally I think I said something like "I'll try this [lying on the couch] today." I think by that time I had decided I *was* nuts and I deserved to be there. But then I was comfortable, and I don't think I ever went back to the chair.

Before analysis there were some irrational things that I would do from time to time. I would just explode. I would take things out on Paula that had nothing to do with her at all. When you say to somebody, "Why the hell can't you turn the light out?" or "*Why* is that refrigerator door open all the time?" you think these are really the problems, that these things are what you're really talking about. You really believe it.

But Mildred would ask, "What else could it possibly be?"—a question you'd never get from anybody else other than a professional. I would say, "It *is* the light." And Mildred would be smart enough to say, "I agree with you, it *is*. But let's make up something. If it wasn't that, what could it be?" You get started this way, at least.

Deep down you just know that you have this need to argue, to squabble, to put down, to hold onto the past. You've decided that there's nothing wrong with you but there's something wrong with your wife. If only she would behave, everything would be all right. "How could she behave that way in public? How could she behave that way here?" It's always she, she, she. And you think, "Oh, if I hadn't gotten married, I wouldn't have any of these problems."

That's how it is. It's like you've got this big problem on your hands and there's no way out. Before you go through therapy, one of the things is that you don't have any alternatives. You seem locked into certain situations, locked into a way of behaving. You have no idea what you're going to do with yourself. It's a long time before you get around to knowing that.

You spend some of your day with this funny kind of feeling which I later identified as guilt. The guilt came from thinking I had made this arrangement with my mother, and my father would find out about it. It's thinking your father is weak when actually he's very strong. But you have to cut him down to size: it's the only way you know how to deal with this huge man who can just eliminate you in a second if he feels like it.

It's the basic, classic situation, and what's so interesting is that *because* it is that situation, you reject it. You say, "Are you kidding? That's the most ordinary thing I ever heard of. So it isn't that. I have something else the matter with me, I'm sure." And you talk about everything else under the sun until you get back to this again.

And of course you don't want to talk about it, because you've got your little plans. No one's going to take these secrets away, and no one's going to change this nice setup you've developed in which you're going to stay with Mommy, and Daddy isn't going to find out about it. You're going to be Mr. Innocent and all that.

It's amazing. Both my parents are dead, but I've come to this fabulous understanding of them. And I only wish my father had lived longer. Although we had a terrific relationship—the bad relationship was the secret one in my mind—I would have been more comfortable, less anxious in the relationship we were having anyway had I got rid of all this garbage. That would have been something nice.

All my energy was spent in keeping this knowledge about my private thoughts and plans away from my father. But it came through. It always comes through, because when you're trying to hide something, it always comes out. Wanting to kill him and all kinds of things. It comes out in the form of screaming and yelling, putting him down and blaming him for things. That actually happened. That's how the little boy was behaving when he *was* a little boy. The problem is how this situation invades the present and influences your behavior.

By not actually dealing with the past, I was letting the past control the present. And so there was no present. I would have a fight with someone at a party and not know why. I would think, "Why did I get into an argument over Red China?" There wasn't any reason. We'd be coming back from the party and I'd say, "I have no idea what happened there."

The main thing that got me to go into analysis was the opening night of the play *The Star-Spangled Girl.* I felt I wasn't good the opening night, even though I was good every other night. Well, opening nights are never the same as any other night, so something's going to be different anyway. But I didn't know that. And I kept bringing up the fact that I had been a little off on opening night and driving Paula nuts. And it depressed me terribly.

What it had to do with was the fact that everybody was watching; it was the most important night, and I had to keep myself small. There's some little trigger inside of you that says, "I'm not going to throw the pass well because they'll all see. I can throw it in practice but not at this moment." Why? Because you can't allow your father to see that you're big and successful and can do this. You've spent your whole life playing the game in which you say, in effect, "I'm nothing, I'm innocent, I can't do anything, so I can't possibly take this woman (my mother) away from you." You're saying, "Don't worry about me; I'm just a little kid." This is the guise you must have for him.

But you can't understand this situation the first day you're in analysis and say, "Oh, I see. I'm much better now, thank you." You have to hear it over and over, and you have to come at it from every which way. It's only after a long time that you actually get at it, actually believe it. I used to fight it in every way and believe that it was just a bunch of words. But, to me, dreams are something basic; they don't lie. And there were too many dreams that kept pointing in this direction for me to say to Mildred, "It's just a bunch of your words."

Analysis involves a great deal of pain, and sometimes I thought, "Why go there every day and open this wound up and cause all this pain? Why not just not go? Why bother with this?" There were lots of times when I'd go to analysis feeling really great and just get in the outer office and then become so angry I couldn't see straight. I'd say, "I was fine until I got up there and somebody said something or I looked at a magazine and read something." But you can't walk around with blinders on and not go out of the house simply because you don't know what you're going to meet out there that's going to ruin your day.

But I would be affected by these things that were happening to me. I'd go out and somebody would open his door in such a way as to dent my car. I'd interpret this as a personal punishment. I'd blame myself for being at the wrong place at the wrong time.

Or if I didn't like the way I dealt with someone, I'd say, "I should have said such-and-such; why didn't I?" I would blame myself for things.

If I got a bad review, there was no possibility that the critic could be wrong. I'd think I deserved the bad notice. If it was a good review, it didn't mean too much to me. I'd think, "That critic must be a fool." As Mildred would say to me, "You don't want to be in a club that would have you as a member."

I wasn't too crazy about myself, and that was very hard for Paula to take. She liked me, and the person she liked didn't like himself—which made her feel bad.

Now I like myself, for the most part. It's a process that's almost intangible, really. Everything changes. Your day changes. Everything's more awake and alive. You deal with other people on a straighter level.

Now my dreams don't seem to be so intellectual. They are more passionate. They seem to be richer emotionally. I also think I enjoy my fantasies more. I have them more fully and freely without feeling guilty about them.

I began my analysis in late 1967 or 1968 and continued with it until 1974. But we were always away [from New York], so I would say I was only involved in the analysis for about six months of each year. So my total time in analysis was about four years.

I never thought my analysis was harming me, but I sometimes thought it was a lot of crap and I'd be glad to be out of it.

But I needed Mildred, and she was so extraordinarily helpful in the midst of what seemed—at the time—like terrible crisis that I had the same kind of feeling that you have with your mother (which, of course, is the type of figure the analyst is supposed to be): I'm leaving home but I'm not going to cross the street because I need the protection, the warmth and the affection. I need all these things, so how far am I going to go? So there was always this ambivalence.

When we moved out to California, it was a little difficult not seeing Mildred all of a sudden. I didn't really want to stop. But I don't think we *could* have moved a year earlier. It seemed necessary then for me to go to analysis. Now I actually feel like going back for a while. And, when we're back in New York, we go.

Rod Steiger

"Can I get you anything?" a caftan-draped Rod Steiger asked when I arrived at his white clapboard beach house in Malibu. After leading me into a separate brick structure located outside the residence—and learning that I desired nothing—he headed back into his house. He returned shortly with a large cup of tea and a box of Kleenex for himself.

A Tiffany lamp overhead helped brighten our meeting place, which serves as a retreat where Steiger can work at his desk, take phone calls and review scripts. A built-in wall barbecue, pictures of Steiger in various roles (including Napoleon), a poster advertising *W. C. Fields & Me,* awards, tennis rackets and the contents of six boxes of memorabilia collected by the actor's mother gave this room a sense of both familiarity and function.

"You talk about images," he said, as he pulled an old picture of himself from a group of similarly dated photographs cluttering his desk. "Well, that's me. And if all of a sudden they play a movie that I did fifteen or twenty years ago, I think, 'My God, who is that person?' "

During the course of his sometimes philosophical remarks, Steiger frequently left sentences unfinished and syntax in disarray. Occasionally, he would excuse himself for digressing. But he was a solicitous subject—"Am I helping you?" he would inquire—and displayed a winning warmth under what sometimes passes, to his chagrin, as a gruff exterior.

People go into therapy for different reasons at different ages. At *any* age in your life, the basic problem is a matter of connecting with another person.

I know when I first went to see a psychiatrist it was because I knew a lot of girls but, for some reason or other, I wasn't very happy about the whole thing. And I decided they couldn't all be bad: there must be something wrong with me. I knew a lot of them at a sexual level, but then I still didn't feel satisfied emotionally; I didn't feel fulfilled. And it wasn't because of anybody's sexual inadequacies. It was because I didn't allow my emotional self to get involved with my physical self. I was trying to keep them apart, I guess. I found out I was dividing things into two camps; not letting the mental and the physical go together, so to speak. I wasn't operating as an entity. This was when I was twenty-six.

The analyst helped me understand some of the people with whom I grew up, my mother and my stepfather. He helped me to recognize them as people with problems of their own, rather than as people who should be judged.

One of my parents had an alcohol problem. I didn't like her, I thought, for many years. It was only when I came back from the service and lived with her for a while that I began to judge the person as a human being and not as somebody who failed me—even though, in a sense, I felt that she had.

The basic problem that I had was my trying to be everything unto myself, which is an impossibility. I came from a broken home, so I was trying to be my mother to myself and my father to myself. When I made love to somebody, it really was almost like I was by myself: I wasn't sharing anything emotionally. The psychiatric term is autocratic personality.

No matter what tricks you may play with yourself, you ain't gonna make it by yourself. It's much more fun with somebody else. There is the necessary other half of you, or other person that you need. I never was a group person. I never thought I missed anything. I'm the type of person who'll go to a party even though I just don't feel like going. Then, when I get there, I'll take it over and not even know it. I'll start laughing

and joking and have a great time. My wife will say, "You didn't want to come, and now we can't get you out."

When I first went into analysis, I guess I wanted to get out of it, so right away I asked, "How's this going to interfere with my acting?" And the analyst said, "If you think an increase of knowledge at any level is going to be detrimental to your development as a human being, you need not come back." Well, there's no way you can answer that. So I had to say, "What time can I come back?"

The only thing I thought was bad about analysis in the beginning was the tendency of the new patient to analyze everything, to overanalyze—and I went through this. You have to go through this stage.

When you first go, you tell everything. The big shock, of course, is that after you've described how you want to wipe out half the world—or told how you think half the world doesn't like you—the analyst says, "Well, that's normal; everybody thinks like that." And you say, "What do you mean that's normal? How can you say that?"

I never had any big hysterical problem. I was lucky. I didn't have any functioning problem. I think you should go into therapy for the selfish reason that you think you're missing something. I want to get as much out of living as I can get.

I don't think you should make anything like therapy a refuge. There are those who use it as an escape valve. There are those who'll change doctors because they wear out their mother or father image. Suddenly they begin to see the analyst as himself and go someplace else.

I think if you change your analyst more than three times, you'd better take a good look at yourself. These people who do this are looking for a miracle. They're the ones who don't understand analysis. You have to think of analysis as going to school about yourself. You have to think, "This is just to increase my knowledge and help make my day happier—and that's *all*."

Most people go into therapy looking for a single sentence that's going to be a formula for living the rest of their lives. But

since life is constant change, there can be no single formula.

But it's good to have somebody to talk to once in a while in your life. I went to talk to a doctor just recently when I went through a depression. They say you have crisis years in your life—when you're seventeen, thirty and fifty. Evidently no matter what you've done—whether you've done a lot or a little—you're going to be dissatisfied and start to do that unnecessary summation.

They call it executive anxiety. The doctor said that it's just that you're worried about continuing, you're worried that you haven't done enough, you're worried that you're not appreciated, and you're worried that you'll be forgotten. It's all the things that everybody worries about and everybody seems to go through.

It all started because I didn't feel good. I worked very hard on *W. C. Fields & Me*—I guess a little too hard—so I was tired and went into a depression. I thought there was something wrong with me physically. You begin to think all kinds of ridiculous things. So I went down to Scripps to have a complete checkup, and I passed everything with flying colors.

I was imagining maybe I had ulcers. You can actually psych yourself out. I got so anxious that I would do dumb things. I remember once I asked five people to dinner at a little Italian restaurant over here in Malibu. Well, I thought I was going to faint during the entire dinner. Now there was no way I was going to faint, but I had convinced myself somehow that I was going to pass out. I don't know why I should have been anxious about the dinner; I mean, everybody at the table was a good friend of mine.

Another reason I went to Scripps is that there's no doubt that you can have a lot of trouble with hypertension brought on by your mental state. Until somebody begins to talk to you and you begin to examine your mental state together, you're tense and your blood pressure goes up—and when you're fifty years old, that ain't good.

Another thing about the fifty-year-old crisis is that people begin to think about death much more than when they were thirty or thirty-five. And also you begin to use phrases that

you've never used before, like "I can't wait that long anymore." And it depresses you the first time you hear yourself say that. In my profession I keep reading a lot of crappy scripts looking for a good one. When I did *The Pawnbroker* I had waited fourteen months—during which I didn't work—and I turned down a lot of junk and a lot of money. Well, it's a fact: I can't afford to wait fourteen months anymore. And these things begin to bother you.

I go to see a man now—I talk to him maybe twice a week—because this depression was just this year [1976]. I don't like it. I kind of resent it a little bit, because I say, "Jesus, here I am fifty years old: what is this—can't I learn anything?" But you also learn it's a different person than it was last time. Twenty-four years have gone by; something's gotta have changed, for Christ's sake. And with new growth, there are new problems. I have problems now I never had years ago. Years ago I had certain goals. Now all of a sudden you find you've accomplished those goals and you're wondering why you don't quite feel satisfied. I have won the English Oscar twice, the German Oscar, the Italian Oscar and the American Oscar. And sometimes I look at them on days when I don't feel I like what I'm doing and wonder, "What's it all mean?"

In a sense a good actor is very close to being an analyst. The difference, I think, is that the analyst is intellectually aware of what he's dealing with: he can talk about ids and egos. The actor doesn't know these things but he can feel them and use them to create another person. The analyst, in a sense, creates another person out of you: a more balanced person. The true actor creates another human being, too, except one who doesn't really exist—or at least exists only temporarily, while the actor is manufacturing him, so to speak.

I became pretty good friends with the first analyst I went to. The only thing was that years later—and this kind of shocked me—he came over to my house, and as he was leaving he handed me something and said, "This is for you." And I asked, "What is it?" "Well," he said, "I've written this movie script." But this was after I was no longer a patient.

You have to realize an analyst is a human being. That's why

when I did a picture called *The Mark*, in which I played an analyst, I made him a chain smoker, a coffee drinker, and a man who had trouble with his own girl friend.

Very few people have any understanding of what acting's all about. So when the analyst would start talking about acting—something I knew that he didn't know about—I was a little disappointed. Acting is not a business. If it were a business to me, I would have done commercials all my life, and I wouldn't worry about the quality of what I was doing. I'd do television series and get all the money I could and run. So sometimes when the analyst would use the term "show business," it would make me mad.

The funniest thing—and one of the most constructive—an analyst ever said to me was that we all have a tendency to think we're special and we're going to suffer for the world. He said, "I'm going to ask you a question, and I just want you to say 'yes' or 'no.' " I was surprised because he never put things like that. He said, "This is just a game. Do you think you're Jesus Christ?" So I said, "No." He said it took me fifteen seconds to say "No." He said it took five seconds to get over the shock of the question and five seconds to say "No," but how did I account for those other five seconds? And I had to laugh.

He said all people think they have to save the world when they're young and romantic. But you can't save it. You just straighten yourself out, and that will contribute toward saving it. You contribute on your little level. Don't picture yourself as King Kong saving the world. (You'd be surprised how much King Kong comes up in an analyst's office. It's a quick way of saying things. It's not the macho thing at all. It looks like that in the beginning, but it isn't. It refers to challenging the whole world and feeling you're going to win. But, as also was pointed out, King Kong didn't win, if you remember the end of the movie. Somehow we just remember him standing up there at the top of the Empire State Building and forget that we knocked him off.)

In therapy I found out that at certain times I would condemn myself because I didn't want to realize that perhaps someone I

was deeply involved with in my life was not good for me. So, rather than face that, I'd think there was something wrong with me. Or, the other way around, I'd find myself condemning the other person because I didn't want to face the fact that I had an inadequacy.

Also in therapy you begin to see more of what you really are. And all of a sudden you learn things; it isn't wrong to lose your temper—given that things are justified—and it isn't wrong to get upset. Who said it was wrong? And why use the word "wrong" anyway? The only thing I know is that to hurt somebody unnecessarily is wrong. The other thing you have to learn is that sometimes you may have to upset somebody for the preservation of your own happiness. For example, one of the hardest things in the world is to say "Goodbye." But at a certain time you find out that you have to cut off your relationships with certain people in your life.

If you're involved with a person to whom you constantly give, give, give, when you get upset and angry, one of the reasons is that you're worrying about their happiness; but, on the other side of it, you're really saying, "Why the hell don't they ever worry about mine?" I say as a joke—but it isn't a joke—you forgive people two times, and the third time you kill—or get out. Otherwise you must be a masochist.

One of the most difficult things to do sometimes, in a sense, is get out of bed. It's so easy to lie in bed and moan and groan to yourself. The bed is like a big womb or something. I know when I went through a great depression, Jeez, I would stay in bed ten or twelve hours, and it didn't bother me at all. I loved it. I'd read.

I think we've gotten very indulgent. We overmedicate ourselves, we overanalyze ourselves; and if there's anything wrong, we run in six different directions.

But you had better call somebody besides a friend the first time you wake up in the morning and say "I don't care anymore" or "What difference does it make?" Or if you begin to bounce from person to person, bed to bed, bar to bar or job to job.

Don't go to other people's shrinks. Call up a university and say, "I think I'd like to have some help in understanding myself. Are there a couple of doctors you can recommend?" Then you go to see the people they recommend. One of them you will like, and that's the one you start out with.

I remember when one had the wrong idea of strength and the last thing one would do was admit one was having a depression. "Not me; I'm all right. I'm man enough," one might say. Now I think it's marvelous to be able to say to someone, "Listen, not only are we friends on the tennis court, we're friends the rest of the time, too. I feel shitty, so would you like to come and have a cup of coffee with me?" The other person must realize that the worst thing he can do is advise you. What he needs to do is listen.

One thing I used to do in analysis that wasn't good was try to figure out a reason why a person did something terrible—so you finally wind up excusing him. Only lately, in the last five years, will I say, "This is not a good man." Up to that time I thought there was no such thing as evil in the world. Then, all of a sudden, I said, "Wait a minute, this guy is evil. He waits, he calculates, he makes friends, and all the time he is trying to push something." I think anybody who uses the emotions and time of other people's lives purely to gain material things for himself, or a sense of power, is, to me, rather a feeble and destructive human being.

There's a certain amount of pain in any growth. People are supposed to be unhappy in their lives from time to time. You're not supposed to have eternal happiness: it would be a definition of monotony. Discomfort and unhappiness have brought forth probably most of the progress of mankind.

You have to realize that to be satiated completely is to be dead. Life is kind of a glorious treadmill, but it *is* a treadmill. But there ain't any other thing, so you might as well try to enjoy it as much as you can. Which may sound kind of depressing—but it isn't. Struggle is maybe the most important necessity in life, because only when you've struggled and won do you really understand the pleasure of living.

Unfortunately, we're also the only animal equipped to

dream. Now that is one of our most glorious and tragic gifts of nature. Impossible dreams are necessary to give you the strength to go forward. In front of an acting class I said, "An artist has to have these necessary dreams that will crucify him." To dream costs a lot. To accomplish a dream, though, has a reward that's incredible.

Lee Grant

It was one o'clock in the afternoon—per her instructions—when I arrived at Lee Grant's house on a hill overlooking the Pacific. The Oscar-winning actress was still asleep when her house man showed me in. Forty-five minutes later she descended the stairs from her bedroom, asked if I would like coffee or tea, then disappeared into her kitchen.

Soon she returned, wearing a pale green hostess gown. She sipped coffee as we chatted in a cozy living room with a low wooden ceiling crisscrossed by beams. A Spanish-speaking cook, a cat, two dogs and Grant's young daughter wandered through the room from time to time, but nothing seemed to interfere with her concentration, even when she would break off our conversation momentarily to kiss her child or offer a warm word.

"Everything about myself has always bothered me," said the woman who credits her first therapist with "starting a new life for me." Her odyssey since her initial contact with psychotherapy has been a fascinating one, filled with both personal discovery and professional accomplishments on stage and in such films as *Shampoo* and *Voyage of the Damned.*

My first experience with therapy was in New York, when my marriage to my first husband was in trouble. I found my psychiatrist through a friend of ours, [screenwriter] Walter Bernstein. I went to the same man he had gone to, because at that time I was blacklisted, and I wanted to go to a doctor who would understand my politics. I didn't want to have to go through explaining the reasons why I had taken the positions I had, because my problems were in another area entirely.

So I went to Alex Thomas, who I think is the head of Mt. Sinai. He helped me get through each day. It was a therapy that was geared toward helping you accomplish various tasks in life—like driving, crossing the street, paying your bills and making dinner. It gave me the ability to handle practical tasks that I could hang onto, so that I wouldn't fall back into anxiety attacks.

Alex had a theory—from working with soldiers in World War II—that the amount that people know about themselves does not help them to change. The thing which helps people to change, according to his theory, is the process of changing, the actual actions that force you to change.

That basically fit in very well with a pragmatism that I have, since I'm basically action: I do something, and either I survive my action or I die. At this point I've had many survivals and many deaths on the basis of my actions.

At the time I saw Alex, I guess I was having a nervous breakdown—I think. I was going into depressions. The world out there had been an enemy of mine for twelve years. The boundaries of my own world were very circumscribed at that time. It was a boundary of just this apartment that I lived in. There was no answer in the house, and there didn't seem to be an answer outside of it, so I was really stuck in between.

Alex forced me to take small actions each day to keep from encouraging the depression, to keep from feeding on it. And when a job came up, he urged me to take it, to get out into the world. He urged me to do this even though it meant breaking up with my husband. He forced me to take this job which meant leaving for California and going three thousand miles away and staying away for three months. It was a play that was traveling across the country. I didn't see how I could do it; I didn't see how I could leave my apartment. I had been very much in love, and the things I did, the places I went, were very circumscribed for a very long time.

But Alex said, "You will not die." It meant everything, those simple words, because we don't realize what we really think is going to happen. It was not really a question of doing a play; it was a question of leaving what I cared most about. And to be told very simply that I could do it and live was the most reassuring thing.

So I took the job, and it was the opening of this whole new period for me; it was like crashing through a window and getting to the other side. So this psychiatrist was very instrumental in starting a new life for me.

Taking care of day-to-day things—which was something Alex helped me with—always was and continues to be an area in which I'm a blunderer. It's like my fingers fall into some prehensile shape—because they can't do things. The simplest things have always been done for me. Money has always been handled for me, first by my parents, next by my first husband, and then by various business managers. So for me, at the age of thirty, the idea of opening up a bank account and keeping records was like a whole new world. It gave me a tremendous feeling of accomplishment.

Before my first marriage I had never cooked, so now I *love* the kitchen. Making something and having people eat it is a very big thing to me because it came so late in life. I have a big theory about that: I love things that come late in life, and I've always tried to delay. When I was little I used to put the thing I loved most to eat last, with dessert. Like I loved lamb chops when I was in high school, and they always came last. And it's the way I feel in life. I don't *want* all I can get now; I never have. It's like I want something to look forward to. I want to know the dessert is still out there somewhere.

Until this year—and I've lived out here for nine years—I didn't drive, which put a tremendous burden on the studios and friends. I was afraid of getting lost. I was afraid of what would happen if I got off a certain route, which was like a little square that I had always driven: down the Pacific Coast Highway and left on Sunset to the Beverly Hills Hotel. I thought that if I went up on a side street I'd be swallowed up someplace and never be able to get back again—which was irrational but which was the fear I had to act on.

Now the funny thing is this: by strangers I meet outside of myself, I am considered a very strong person. I'm *amazed* at how many people have that image of me. And it's not totally inaccurate. I mean, I've taken great risks all my life—and known what I was doing—and paid for them. I'd come out for every cause, everything I believed in that was unpopular. That was not pleasant. I don't enjoy going against the tide. So as weak as I was about the driving, that's how strong I am in other areas, where I've had no compunction at all about risking and feeling absolutely certain and contented with those risks.

So I'm like a double person: it's a paradox. And I don't know where the weaknesses are going to be. I *do* know where the strengths are by this time. And I guess it's the strength in me that leads me constantly to overcome the other part of myself. I'm not sure which part is the source of the talent. What I do know is this: there's a child in every actor I've ever known. That child—who causes so much trouble for them and who's fat usually and unattractive and frightened—is also the source of tremendous insight, because that frightened, deprived child is also very insightful about the problems of other people, and that enables him to act out the lives of other people.

I've always been terrified of going on stage. This fear, which concerns me the most, is one amidst many other fears that are small. At any rate, my theory has always been that if I get a fascinating little part which lets me hide most of the time and lets somebody else carry the show, I can get away with it. This was the whole principle behind picking the shoplifter in *Detective Story*, as it was the smallest part in the play. The fact that it ran away with the Cannes Film Festival, an Academy Award nomination and the Critics Circle award was so devastating to me and so immobilizing that I didn't go on stage after that for a long time.

I was asked to return to the stage in *The Prisoner of Second Avenue*, and I did. I felt it was time for me to take the kind of step that would make me grow, deal with my fears and solve them. It was a very hard year for me, partly because we couldn't be together as a family and partly because a lot of the feelings I had accumulated couldn't be released in the play. Lots of times when you have fears or needs, you're in a vehicle in which they can come out. But in *Prisoner*, the man is the one who has the nervous breakdown, so I was very jealous: *I* wanted to have it. I needed it, and I think it would have made a great difference in my life if I'd been able to release those feelings on stage, rather than playing the strong, supportive character, which was not what I felt.

So there was a kind of tension that I couldn't release on stage, couldn't release with my family, which was not there, or my best friends, who were here in California. So I didn't have that many people to communicate with. There was a building up of tension and a tremendous desire for the whole thing to end. I began to feel like a prisoner myself: I was counting the days until I was finished with the play, till I could be released and start on something else.

The last week of the play I came on in the second act—playing opposite Peter Falk—and I couldn't think of one of the words of my monologue. I went totally blank. I excused myself, went backstage and looked at the script. When I looked at the words on the printed page, they had absolutely no reality for me at all. This is the nightmare that every actor has had.

Everybody said, "Well, of course, everybody forgets lines." And I know this, but I don't permit myself these mistakes. It's not other people who don't permit you things, and that's one of the things you find out in therapy. It's not the audience who is my enemy, it's myself; it's the person in me who doesn't permit me any kind of humanity, any kind of human error.

Well, of course, what I had after that experience was a terrible kind of self-disgust and a determination never, ever to go on stage again. What had happened really kind of relieved me and released me from any obligation ever to go on stage again after I was finished with that last week.

And then I realized that there were fewer and fewer things I was permitting myself to do: I was not driving, and now I was not performing on stage. I was as limited here in California almost as I had been in New York. The circumferences of the things I was permitting myself to do were getting smaller and smaller. I would rarely go out to parties—it was only the people who came to the house that I would see—so that instead of expanding, as I had started to do when I left my husband, I was beginning to live the narrowest existence I had ever lived.

And I made up my mind that I would get some help out here on all these little rules and regulations I had made for myself that meant that I could not do these things: I could not get up before twelve, I could not go to bed before four, and I couldn't drive anyplace.

I started inquiring about doctors. I was determined to go back on stage, too, at some time or other, because I used to ride horses when I was little, and I knew that the same law—which is that when you're kicked off, you get right back on again—applied absolutely. I knew that I had to go back on stage or else—knowing how I had gone nine years without driving in California—it would be that long before I acted, and I would nurse all the weaknesses in myself, which is what my tendency is.

My experiences with the first two men I saw were bummers. This was the last thing I had expected to go through, because my experience with Alex had been so good. Whether I was with him or not—and many years I wasn't—I could call him up when I was in trouble. Just knowing he was there when I hit a pit would be very important to me.

The first man I saw in L.A. was very warm and very fatherly. I have a suspicion of fatherly people in that there is always the authoritarian side to the father. At one point I was explaining something to him and he said, "Now you see how feminine you are? That's the way it should be." And I said, "That's a very weird thing to say to me; that's a very strange choice of words. You like me when I'm like a child, like a little girl."

I think at one point, when he was going away, I said, "Oh,

do you really have to go? I'm so sorry." And he put his arms around me, which made me very uncomfortable, because we were alone in the office and because we were very close. And I certainly feel that it could have been—from him—just the most simple expression of affection, the kind of affection that anyone gives anybody who's leaving. But this incident raised feelings and worries in me that I felt I had to talk about with him. I didn't feel that we should be close physically. There were enough things that I couldn't handle without even *wondering* about whether I was right or wrong. And I'd certainly give him the benefit of the doubt. But when I raised the issue with him he got very angry.

There were things I was doing at that point that I felt that he as a doctor should be very encouraging about. I had just received a copy of an article I had written for the *New York Times*, and I gave it to him. I felt very good about it. I think I had gotten more response from other people on that article than almost anything else I'd done. And he just dismissed it.

At the same time, I was asked to direct a special on television. It was a great challenge that I was very excited by, but he saw it as a threat to the therapy. He kept saying, "When are you going to lie down on the couch?"—because I wouldn't; I would only sit in the chair. And he would ask, "When are you going to commit yourself to seeing me four times a week?" I couldn't understand why he wouldn't encourage the kind of outside activity that used the strongest part of me, the healthiest part.

He became very punishing in terms of being angry with me very often, particularly with my not being there on time because I was working down at the studio with these women. I would arrive at his office maybe five or ten minutes late, and the session would then be about my lateness instead of using the time for whatever else there was.

He put it to me that if I cared enough about the therapy, I would give up the work on the outside and dedicate myself simply to getting on the couch and going into things—which really took me aback. Because the whole principle of my first therapist was to encourage the highest degree of outside activity I could possibly have. This second therapist was saying, "Give up the work; give up everything you have to do and just come here and be a patient."

I said, "No matter how late I am, I pay for the time, and even it there's only fifteen minutes, it's time that I've paid for."

He said, "Be here tomorrow at 6:30," and I tried very hard. I was probably there at 6:35. I waited in the little waiting room, that cubicle, and when forty-five minutes had gone by, I knocked on the door to his room. There was no answer, and I realized that I had been sitting there forty-five minutes alone in that building. I couldn't believe it. I went down and called his house. I said, "Have you forgotten I was supposed to see you?" And he said, "You were five minutes late." There's no point repeating the conversation, because I realized that he was a man who had to punish. It was absolutely shocking to me that a person whom one must trust in order to continue could use his own problems to get the kind of control over a patient that he felt he must have.

I looked around for another doctor. I was at a party at which there was a doctor somebody said I must see. The doctor seemed very pleasant and said, "Come and see me and we'll talk." So I went, had a session with him and then got a bill for seventy-five dollars. I talked to him about it. I said, "I think you should tell people ahead of time that this is what you charge, because actors can't pay this kind of money—and I can't." So he showed me his degrees. I told him, "Yes, but I have a tremendous sense of money with you, and I live in a community [among actors] where people give help to each other free." Well, everybody should be paid for his services, but I had a feeling that [patients] were paying for things that people couldn't afford in the first place, like houses in Beverly Hills. This man had a way of life which the problems of his patients were supporting—which was insupportable to me as a philosophy.

So I finally ended up with the doctor I'm with now, who was recommended by a woman doctor. He's been very consistent and very dependable. This analyst saw me through *The Seagull* in Williamstown—when I went back on the stage—*The Little*

Foxes here in L.A., and the period when I was doing my series, *Fay*.

That first night when I went back on stage in *The Seagull* I almost can't describe what it was like forcing myself to get out there.

On top of everything else, I have a block on names, which came from my old House Un-American Activities days, when they asked you to give the names of friends. As a result, after my appearance in front of the committee, I promptly forgot every name I ever knew. So that when I see people I've known for ten years, I cannot say their names; I cannot introduce them. I think it's nature's way of preventing you from being a stool pigeon.

At any rate, there were two people I had to introduce in *The Seagull*, and my whole concentration was in going over their names again and again, because I knew that when the moment came, I might forget.

The rehearsal period is always the best time for me. It's such a release; I'm so free in rehearsal. But the sense of performance in front of an audience is like getting up in front of a class in school, at which I was always terribly inadequate. It's like coming through with my lessons and having to be correct. Of course, [to me] what the audience is really asking is for me to do for them what I did in rehearsal, because it would be a revelation.

What you want on stage is the permission to do something over if you don't like it; in other words, permission to make a mistake. *Fay* was comparable to the rehearsal situation, because when you do a filmed half-hour television comedy, most of the time it's the camera that makes a mistake. There isn't that sense of doom that if you don't get it right this one time, you're just not going to get it.

Most of the actors I know—no matter how well established they are, no matter what work they've done—are virgins where the next play or film is concerned, if it really means something to them. The last piece of work one does feels like it's twenty years ago, like it's something that has nothing to do with you anymore. When people talk about it, there's a strange sense of distance. It's only this "Can I do it again?" I don't mean that a part of you doesn't say, "Of course I can do it." I'm just saying there *is* this element in all actors.

Therapy forced me to drive. The drive to the doctor's office was so long—an hour going in and an hour coming back, three times a week—because I was afraid to take the freeway. The fact that, with a little courage, I could use the freeway and make the trip in thirty-five minutes just solved the problem for me. The freeway had been a big fear of mine because I was always afraid I'd get killed. And once I accomplished the freeway, leaving my little square and going to people's houses that I hadn't been to became something that I kind of got interested in. I remember once I was on my way to Mike Nichols's house to see his wife—their baby had just been born—and I got lost. I stopped at a house that turned out to belong to a very well known guitarist, who was very friendly, gave me an album and told me how to find Mike Nichols's place. And I realized then that getting lost could also be finding other things and other people.

When you've lost your fear of something after nine years—as I did with my driving—then of course you become entirely intrepid. I'm a maniac on the highway now. There's no place I won't go, no place I can't go. The fact that this has happened is proof to me that you can not only fight fears but overcome them and start to enjoy and take pleasure in the very thing you previously feared.

So I keep thinking that this will happen with my work on stage and that one day I'll have a wonderful time with it. I do that on talk shows now. The first time I did a talk show—it was with Dick Cavett in New York—I can't tell you what it was like. The only way I got out on that stage is that someone pushed me. And Cavett had to come take me over to the seat because my legs wouldn't move, the terror was so great. I think I was more afraid of doing talk shows—of getting up as myself—than in any other situation. And now I have no fear of it.

The only time I was obsessed with sexual discussion in therapy was before I did *Shampoo*. Somehow it always translates in terms of my work. I have a very good thing going with my husband, but going out into another sexual situation—which is what I had to do in *Shampoo*—was like being given the job of having an affair. When you're acting, all you can use is yourself—that's your instrument. My poor doctor would get very confused when I would talk about these sexual problems which had to do with a part. He would keep asking me, "Is this a part or is this you?" And I would say, "I don't know." It opened up the area of affairs, and it was something I had to go into, because the woman I was playing was somebody whose whole release was through going to bed with one man after another. And my problem was to go to bed with Warren (Beatty). And there was a real problem in that, in the story, I had been going to bed with him for *months*, so it was supposed to be very free and very uninhibited. But the fact was that as friends and fellow actors, we had *not* been to bed. Getting into bed with a fellow actor—in front of cameras and a director—was opening up virginal feelings in me that were very wrong for this woman I played, who *did* it all the time, who was aggressive about it and simply wanted to have her sexual needs satisfied and get on with it. And I didn't know how to get to that point. So my therapist and I discussed it very much. I would say it opened great areas of lust in me at that point, because I just found everybody who walked by me so attractive that I couldn't bear it.

Psychoanalysis is a new area for me in that I've never been in it before. I'll tell you the truth: I don't know whether it works or whether it doesn't. Somehow I have a resistance to [the idea of the] subconscious. I have a resistance to all kinds of things that can't be explained here and now.

I never realized the kind of role a therapist is supposed to play in your life, as taking the place of a mother or father. It's never happened to me this way, even with my first doctor. I'd go to my therapists for help on a specific problem and I'd know who they were very well. I have a great sense of people fulfilling a certain function and a great resistance to being dependent on them for anything outside of that function. So I don't transform them into lovers. . . . Maybe that's something that's wrong; maybe that's something that gets in the way for me. I don't have this thing called transference, in other words.

The most difficult thing is the fact that I don't know whether my analyst is a person who is entitled to my confidences. There is a judging that goes on in me—that I haven't gotten rid of yet—as to whether this person is wise enough or enlightened enough to be entrusted with my confidences—because I don't think many people are.

The roots of certain of my problems are in my childhood, but they're very mysterious to me and they seem to be beyond my grasping. There is a revelation that I have yet to have about the cause of all my behavior. Sometimes I get a flash and I see it kind of clearly, but I don't understand why I act the way I do—and I would like to. I think there's a great deal in me that I not only keep locked up from my doctor but that is *really* locked off from me.

Paul Michael Glaser

Thirty-five million people watch Paul Michael Glaser on his top-rated *Starsky and Hutch* TV show each week, and the scene as we sat in his Pace Arrow van on location in L.A.'s Century City suggested that a hefty chunk of the audience is probably female. A stream of women—from young to middle-aged—tapped on the window at Glaser's back, while a few of the more venturesome ones actually knocked on the door and requested autographs.

Glaser, whose fans know him as a hip cop named David Starsky, endured these intrusions with relative grace and good humor, although he concurred when one teenager who had asked for his signature volunteered that she was making a nuisance of herself.

His video partner, David Soul, also poked his head in—to pull a few bottles of beer from Glaser's mobile refrigerator and exchange a few words with him about the next show to be shot.

The TV series that is the source of Glaser's fame is also, he told me, the reason for much of the pain he discusses when he visits his psychiatrist.

My dealings with *Starsky and Hutch* and the pressures connected with it are what led me to experience the pain which ultimately led me into therapy.

I was so enmeshed in my work and with the day-to-day getting it done—with that whole tornado of feelings and events going down—that I don't believe I was aware of anything except the pain. All I knew was that I was waking up at three or four or five in the morning with excruciating pain in my stomach. It was fucking going spastic; my colon was going spastic. Everything was just holding on for dear life. Now my stomach is very much under control. Now all the pain's coming out. And I live in great fear that I will lose the love and affection of the public which so adores the lovable David Starsky that I've created. I have to bear the responsibility for that and press on. If that's what happens, that's what happens.

Right now in my life I find more of my creativity going on in therapy than I do in my work, in the sense of getting in touch with who I am, experiencing who I am. With this piece of shit that I do—the series—I experience a lot of anger, a lot of fear, a lot of frustration and a lot of disappointment—all of which are reactions to a thwarted desire to love and be loved.

They are lovely people that I work for, but I sorely miss the *confrontation*. That's a word that's been popping up in my mind lately. There's a confrontation that goes on in therapy and in a one-to-one relationship with your lady that you don't have in this fuck-ass business. People melt into the woodwork, they don't want to confront, they don't want to get it on. It's all well and good for me to understand that I have to learn how to confront and embrace *myself*, but the child in me still wants very much to be able to confront other people and be held by other people, loved by other people. One of the things I have difficulty in learning is to be satisfied with a dialogue about yesterday's football game and just accept that for what it is and go on. But I am looking for levels of passion, and it's part of a testing procedure that I have developed subconsciously to find out if people really are my good friends.

The greatest fear is that you don't exist, that you're not there. In my childhood and in my upbringing probably there was not much substantiation of the fact that I was there. So I had to find other ways. Ergo, I became an actor, seeking approval, the limelight, attention. I still am driven considerably in that way.

I had an absentee father. He was too busy building his own career to be there for me. Mother was dealing with that fact and overcompensating for it, making him into a wonderful superman figure that I have to live up to. I've been looking for a father for a long time, and I imagine I'll continue to look for an even longer time. I'm slowly getting to the point where I'm beginning to become the father, also, to my own child.

My father and I have become pretty good friends now, which is nice. I haven't seen him now for six months, but I'll be seeing him this weekend, and it'll be interesting to see what's gonna happen. At the present time I'm suing Spelling and Goldberg [the producers of *Starsky and Hutch*] to get out of this show. On my part this is a thrust against the authoritarian figure. The child in me is doing it for attention, the adult for artistic reasons. So I'm in quite a bit of turmoil right now; in fact, every minute of my day is in turmoil, and I'm just kind of hanging on by my fingernails. So it'll be interesting to see how I react to my father.

In every relationship I have—particularly in every male relationship—I seek that person to be there for me. I'll give you a case in point. This television show that I do is about a great partnership, a brotherly love between two guys who would die for one another.

So I look at the show and say that within the bounds of television we can make it a hell of a lot better if we do such and such. My partner agrees; we try doing such and such for a period of time, but we keep getting fucked around, jerked around. Finally I realized that the only way you get them to do anything—these people who don't want to give a fuck about human beings and who only care about money and bureaucratic power—is to get 'em where it hurts: tell 'em you're not coming to work until they give you what you want.

So I turn to my partner and I say, "Come on, let's do it." It's an act of faith, of trust, of unanimity. But he says—because of his needs and his space—"I can't do that." The resentment, the anger, the bitterness, the sorrow I feel is boundless—and it has to do with the fact that he was not there for me. I have to deal with that every day. I suppose I could confront him with it, but it hurts too much. I'm afraid I'd fall apart; I'm afraid I'd disappear; I'm afraid of a million things. I need to understand and not personalize, to realize that it's his trip, not my trip. But it's very hard for me to do this, because we're working together, and things we do are in spite of, because of, for and against the other person. It impairs the trust.

People look me in the eye and say, "Well, if you stayed in the show for another year or two, you'd make just tons of money"—what they call "fuck-you money." But I get very panicky that I wouldn't be able to do it. I don't think I'd come out of it a whole person. I've heard so many stories and seen so many people drink excessively and do excessive dope in a series situation because they have to kill the pain; they have to cope. I can't do that. Physically I can't do it; my body will not allow it. And so I find the taxes I pay and the things I do to cope are emotional moves. My novocaine is one of anger. And I couldn't stay angry for that long.

I think I decided to get out of the show in spite of my sessions rather than because of them. If anything—as my therapist explained to me—the optimum situation is to maintain the status quo in terms of the outside world. That way—to make an analogy—you have the clear, calm water of the lake to look down into or to plumb, rather than a lot of choppy waves.

I've been seeing my current psychiatrist for about a year. But I was in therapy once before, when I was in college. It's interesting, because I resisted it very much before I went in this time. When I ended my therapy during college, my prognosis was supposed to have been very good. So I liked to think I could deal with and cope with whatever came down. I'm not sure, but I guess that, partially, going back into therapy this time was an admission that I had not been able to cope and therefore something was wrong. In retrospect, I would have to say that my earlier therapy was not a big success, except to the extent that it helped me get through my life then.

The only time I can think of that I really felt let down in therapy was the first time I saw a psychiatrist. I guess I was about twelve or thirteen. I remember going into his office, and one of the first questions out of his mouth was "Do you masturbate?" Just coming through puberty at that time, it was kind of abrupt and shocking to me—and alienating. I never went to see him again.

Jesus, do you know what I just realized? Thus far I've told you that I've had three experiences with psychiatrists, including the sessions I'm in now. Well, there was another time; I just remembered. Isn't that amazing how you block things out? I was in therapy the first time when I was in private school. All I remember is that the dude was apparently sleeping with a couple of his patients.

One of the things I'm trying to learn in therapy now is not to personalize things so greatly. I have to recognize that things happen around me because they happen and that I am not the cause of them. Rather than relate to the world around me as a giver or withholder of love, I'm trying just to be more curious about it. I find myself just scratching the surface, although the scratches are more like gouges.

What you're dealing with in therapy is a very close relationship with somebody who is familiar with patterns of human behavior. The most important thing for me to do is understand and trust that he's there for me. Now, granted, I'm paying him X dollars an hour to be there for me, for his services—and sometimes I joke about that—but the only other person you can spend that much time with and take so much from without paying him in dollars is your lover or your best friend. And even then you have to realize there are boundaries. With my therapist I can indulge myself if I have to, in the sense of lashing out. I can play the part out all the way. I would like to think I have the freedom to do it in my relationship with my lady—and I do, to a degree—but with the therapist I can indulge the child a bit more.

There aren't as many days when I don't want to go as I thought there would be, or as I was led to believe there would be. As a matter of fact, the psychiatrist's office is a place where I can really get my thoughts together. My working schedule being what it is, I have to deal with so many fucking things that by the time I get finished I welcome the opportunity to be able to go someplace and understand some things about myself and what I'm feeling. I go anywhere from one to three times a week.

I know I could survive without my therapy, but I must say that my creative exercise going down right now seems to have become focused upon working on my own head and keeping my own balance as a person. My acting seems to be very secondary to that.

Therapy is expensive, but I'm making so much money right now that it doesn't mean anything to me. But everything is relative, and the most important thing to me is peace of mind—because I ain't getting any younger. And I didn't have a childhood. If you didn't have a childhood, you spend all your time trying to recapture what you should have had back then. One of the things you have to reconcile yourself to is that you never can have that again. So not only are you having a difficult time existing in the here and now—except in front of the camera—you're having difficulty accepting the fact that today is gone, yesterday is gone, and you're not going to have them again. And there were things I wanted to have when I was ten years old—or five years old—that I will never have. That's my pain, my fear. That's what I relate to as being afraid of getting older: lost moments.

The hardest thing to reconcile with yourself is that the human condition in which you find yourself took thirty-three years to evolve, and it ain't going to take a day, a week, a month or even a year to unravel.

My celebrity status operates to a great degree as a magnifying glass on myself, on the life I'm experiencing, so the highs and lows are magnified.

It's hard for me not to act out my anger and my frustration and instead allow what's underneath—the love and the cry for love—to come out. Most of the time what comes out is anger, which is the cover. This is very difficult for people around me.

There's a whole self-destruct mechanism that goes down. The child is subconsciously seeking proof constantly that he isn't worthy, that he doesn't deserve the love he never got originally. And any proof only substantiates the argument. I knock myself, I tear myself down in my own eyes. I'm very hard on myself and therefore very, very hard on others.

Professionally, I'm very much of a perfectionist. So it's an ironic situation that I find myself in: a lead in a hit series on television, which is the epitome of compromise when it comes down to the artist fulfilling his creative needs.

Another irony is that I've wound up in a situation—with my celebrity status—in which I'm there for a lot of people and in which people *expect* me to be there for them an awful lot. My particular hang-up is that I feel that people expect me to perform—and I have a very difficult time just being.

Look at me. The last thing in the world I need is more support for my vanity or my personalizing process, and yet here I am, an actor, a celebrity, a star, if you will. And this situation just puts me in the limelight even more. What an incredible bed I've made that I have to lie in! I have to find a way to allow that to become humorous to me. When I'm there on the set working, and the shit comes down on me, the humor is lost in the pain still.

I'd like to personalize things less; I'd like to find a more peaceful, constant space for my being; I'd like to learn to enjoy life and being more, and be less compulsive about my work and my life. In doing this I would realize a greater degree of my talent and my self-expression.

The thing I enjoy most is doing a good job when I'm doing one. I enjoy the process of doing the show very much, but I have a hard time owning the rewards, owning the fruits of my labors—although sometimes I allow myself to enjoy the adulation.

The prevailing underlying fear I have is that I don't exist. I can pinch myself, I can eat, and I can fuck. I can do these things and they will tell me I exist. The child's fear is that he doesn't exist. What I try to do in therapy is translate this into specifics. I guess I have a fear that I'm not going to get it together. But I'm trying to learn to make fear a friend and disarm it that way.

Neil Simon

A manservant in a white uniform opened the door to reveal Neil Simon standing in the entrance of his ranch-style house high in the manicured hills of Bel-Air.

There was no waiting routine to endure, because there are no pretensions when Neil Simon gets into the act. His record as America's most successful playwright might make him a logical target for verbal sniping, but one hears only favorable comments. "He is such a nice man," people will tell you, and they are right on the mark.

A latecomer to California, Simon told me, "I've lived here only seven months, and I already feel at home." And so did I as we sat in the playwright's spacious sun-filled living room for an unhurried morning's chat.

Simon's wife, actress Marsha Mason, floated in and out of view, interrupting us once to announce a call from a *Christian Science Monitor* reporter. Picking up the phone by a window that offered a dazzling view of Los Angeles in the distance, Simon courteously reported that he would be busy the remainder of this week, but would the reporter please give him a ring the middle of the next?

Still recovering from a bout with the flu, Simon looked mildly strained but still cut a dapper figure. Wearing a dark shirt, brown knit sweater, light pants and brown loafers, he settled comfortably into a chair, propped his feet on a heavy wooden coffee table and began to talk freely.

I've been through therapy three different times in my life. The first two times were for very different reasons, and I wasn't in long, because I wasn't prepared for it. The first time I went I was twenty-six years old, which was the year after I got married the first time. That was sort of a traumatic time in my life, because I had just ended a working partnership with my brother which had lasted since I was sixteen years old. So when it ended, it sort of threw me into a tizzy. Also, there were all sorts of other problems: my wife and I were newlyweds, and all that.

My main sympton was extreme claustrophobia. If I would get into any kind of an enclosed situation, I would feel awful. Airplanes were the worst place for me and elevators second. So I just thought I would try to see what was the cause of this problem and get relief, because it was horrible not being able to travel anywhere.

Now, years later, I still have claustrophobia minimally. I mean, if an elevator is going to be stopped or trapped I'm going to be uncomfortable, but I realize everyone else will be, too. But I get into airplanes and I have no problems.

It's not through the therapy that I pretty much got over the claustrophobia but through my life, just through getting older and having to deal with a lot of the problems which may have originally caused the fear. There's no one specific reason behind it. Almost everything leads back—as you'll read in all the books—to those first five or six years of your life.

At any rate, when I first went into therapy—when I was working on *The Show of Shows* with Sid Caesar and Imogene Coca—I used to go to the doctor in the morning. It annoyed me because I had to be there at nine o'clock; my session lasted until nine-fifty and I had to be at work at ten. I was the therapist's first patient, and he would often come in late and just deduct the time he missed from the fee. So I would be getting only twenty-five or thirty minutes sometimes. And there were a couple of times he fell fast asleep, which is the ultimate rejection.

So it was awful going to see him. On the days when he was there on time and we *did* go through some heavy trips, I would leave there feeling wiped out but still have to go in to *The Show of Shows* and write comedy.

I continued to see this man for about six months, but the chemistry was not right. First of all, it was not right on my part, because I was not really ready to accept the whole philosophy of it. Also, I didn't think he was a very good doctor. So I didn't go into therapy again for fourteen years.

Then I went because I had reached that critical age in life, forty, when all sorts of strange things start to go on, I guess, in a man's mind.

I felt very troubled, so I saw a second doctor, but I *hated* him; I mean, I truly hated him. So I went screaming from his office—after about three months—saying I'd never go through this again.

I know there are some people who don't get along with their analysts because they don't want to go through the hardship and the work that you go through in analysis. But I just knew that this second doctor was a very, very difficult man to deal with. He was a strict Freudian. He was unbending and ungiving.

My experience with him was right out of a Mel Brooks routine where Brooks is an analyst and he says to the woman [patient], "What is it?" and she says, "Well, I don't want to say, because it's kind of off-color." He says, "Don't be ridiculous; this is analysis, and that's what it's here for; you have to have an open mind," etcetera, etcetera. So the woman tells him what's on her mind and he says, "You are a dirty, filthy pig, and get out of my office. I don't want to see you!"

Well, that's the type of thing, in a way, that my second therapist did. I would tell him some of the thoughts that were going on in my mind, and he would say, "Oh Jesus, you have no sense of morality at all." I knew how wrong he was to say this, and if I had thought he was correct in his judgment, it could have been quite scary. This man was really from the old school in Vienna—and he should have gone right back there.

The only time therapy really meant anything to me was when my wife got ill, four years ago, and I knew she was going to die. It was a very rough time, and I needed some kind of help. I found a woman therapist who has turned out to be the most influential doctor in my life. She is just terrific. I went to her for two and a half years and stopped when we moved out to California from New York. My experience with her made up for all the bad experiences. I still talk to her and call her.

But I'm leaving out the third doctor prior to the lady. When I first got sort of ill as a result of my wife's illness, my own physician said that I really should see somebody, because my blood pressure was getting high.

So I went to see this therapist and I liked him. He was a very intelligent, good man, but he was another strict Freudian, and we didn't seem to really hit it off. There were things about his method that I did not like at all.

For example, you came into his office, and it was a tiny little vestibule with a chair and a screen and you sat behind the screen so that the person coming out wouldn't see you and you wouldn't see him. So you felt like you were in a leper colony. This was really treating us [his patients] as though we were sick people. So you felt guilty about being there.

When I went to the woman therapist, on the other hand, I met lots of my friends there and we sat and talked. There was no stigma. It's the doctor who sets the tone.

The other thing that I objected to about the third doctor was that at that time (when I was seeing him)—when I suddenly had the hypertension and the high blood pressure—I was given diuretics to take, so I had to go to the bathroom much more often than I generally had before.

And this doctor's office was part of his home. So I would say, "I have to go to the john," and he would say, "OK, would you just give me five minutes?" Then he had to clear out his family, clear out all the rooms so that I would go through without being seen by his family or vice versa. So, by going to his bathroom, I was again stigmatized.

So what I would do was either try not to go to the bathroom—in which case I would be sitting there and thinking, "I hope this session's over, because I'm going to pee right on his couch," or just run across the street to the Museum of Natural History and do it there.

While I was seeing this man, I was in a panic one day because things were getting worse and worse with my wife. So I called him up at eleven o'clock one night and said, "I've got to see you, because I'm really in trouble." He said, "Well, I can see you Wednesday at four." Well, I thought, "Fuck yourself." I mean, who needs it by Wednesday at four? I just think this man was not accessible as a human being, so he couldn't be as a doctor, either.

So I went to this man for three months, and I did not enjoy the experience or feel that anything was happening, so I sort of drifted over to this woman. I went to have talks with her, and slowly she became my doctor.

I knew about her because a great many of my friends had gone in, and then my wife, the one who was ill and died, went to her for a short period. Everybody recommended her very highly.

I thought immediately that she would be someone I would stay with, but I had felt that about the man before her, too. When you meet the first day, anybody who comes along with a bandage seems terrific, but over a longer pull, it may well be a different story.

But this woman—Mildred Newman—was wonderful. She wrote *How to Be Your Own Best Friend.* And it occurred to me that if you accept the philosophy of her book, you don't even have to go through therapy. Her philosophy seemed the most unique thing in the world to me, because I didn't know it was OK to like yourself. I had been brought up thinking that liking yourself was a selfish thing: you don't like yourself; you like others. You don't do things for yourself; you do things for other people. I discovered that the more you deny yourself, the more you start to put yourself down and not like yourself, the less chance you have of getting better. So that was the basic thing, I think, that I had to come to learn.

With all the things that kids do, from masturbation to whatever, there come such guilt feelings that you have to say, "Wait a minute, these are not such terrible things I've done, no matter what." Even lying in bed one night and thinking, "I'd like to kill my mother, or kill my father," and picturing the dagger going in their back. You think, "Jesus, what a terrible person I must be." But you learn in therapy that you're not a terrible person, because we all, at times, have these feelings.

I needed those two and a half years with Mildred: first, to get through that period of my wife's illness; then, after she died, I continued going for almost a year because there were lots of other things I had to deal with in my early childhood and background that I did not understand. I still get into problem areas now and then, and when it gets too bad, I may give Mildred a call. Sometimes a conversation on the phone will turn things around for me and help me to think clearly. But I have to keep going back to the basics, which she sort of taught me.

My family was constantly being broken up. It would have been easier if my father had just left and then stayed away: then we would have adjusted to a new life. But he used to come and go and come and go. My parents broke up maybe ten, twelve, fifteen times during my childhood, and each time it seemed final. So my life was on a yo-yo emotionally, because, as a five-year-old kid, I would say,"Oh, terrific, daddy's back and everything's going to be wonderful"; and then, bang, two months later I'd hear the yelling and the screaming and he'd be gone.

They had very violent kinds of fights and things, which was a frightening experience for a kid: you'd put a pillow up to your head to shut it out. It's the worst kind of thing to hear that going on between your parents. Basically that was the most traumatic thing in my childhood.

I felt sort of caught in the middle. You feel like you're double-crossing one parent to like the other because they hated each other so much. And they sort of used this, because one would play me off against the other, as they did with my brother, too. But they did it with me even more, because my brother was older and getting out of it at that time. So I had great guilt feelings about liking or disliking either one of them.

My brother always talked about our home situation like it was a prison and "Someday we'll get out; we'll escape from this place."

My brother, in a way, was a sort of surrogate father, because he was around more than my father and played the paternal role more than my father. He was the encourager in a lot of good ways, the one who encouraged me to become a writer, encouraged my sense of humor, encouraged my athletic ability. My father never did any of these things. He didn't *dis*courage me, either. I knew that he cared for me, but I was very much frightened of him—of his wrath, his anger, his displeasure.

I would never get in my mother's displeasure. She might yell, but I was not afraid of her displeasure.

Being young when I first started therapy and not understanding it, I thought I would go in and I would only divulge a certain amount of information; there were certain things, I thought, that I was not going to tell the doctor.

Also, the first time I went was twenty-two years ago, so there wasn't even the attitude [of today] about being very open. I mean, in our whole lifetime, whoever thought we would get to see pornographic films by just paying money and going in? It was all so taboo. So everything about even your inner thoughts was also taboo, which is why I thought I would just give the therapist the facts but never really tell him what I thought.

To break through that type of thinking is a big deal, and to do it you have to have a lot of confidence in the person you're dealing with. Well, with the first guy, I didn't have this confidence, so I went just so far with him.

The second doctor was a lot more open. Then, finally, by the time I went to Mildred, all guards were down. I mean, I used to look forward to seeing her and talking with her.

When I first went into therapy I figured my humor was all based on the defensive attitude I had toward the world. My way of dealing with things was humor, and I knew that my humor was coming out a lot from my neuroses. So, being very naïve, I said, "Gee, if the doctor cures me, I'm going to lose my sense of humor and I won't be able to write anymore. I will have less impulse, less reason to use this outlet of humor." But this reasoning wasn't true. If anything, therapy enhances your sense of humor, because it gives you a broader perspective on what life is and who you are.

It's up for grabs about what's really the motivating force to begin with. I mean, maybe I did use humor as an outlet as a kid because life was so horrible: the opposite was joy and laughter. As a kid I would to to Chaplin pictures and find that laughing was the best thing that could happen to me, because it wasn't happening at home—so it was what I wanted to spend my life doing. Of course, what you want to do and what you have the talent for is something else: I don't know where the talent comes from.

It makes me remember now how my father used to say to me—and take pride in it—that he was the hardest person in the world to make laugh. And he thought it was a terrific thing, like saying "I don't cry" as some indication of strength. So my father laughed very seldom at comedians—there were only one or two who really broke him up—so that would also have been instrumental in my saying, "Jesus, I'm going to make him laugh one day by becoming a comedy writer." It amazed me to find out how many people there are like that.

There are so many people I know who could use help—like both my mother and my father during their lives—but I don't really think they would have been able to cope with it or deal with it. I don't think they had the intellectual capacity to deal with it. I don't think you necessarily have to be overly intelligent to go through analysis, but you have to have a desire to grow, and most of the people I know who are in trouble don't have that desire. It's like they say, "Leave me alone; I'm OK the way I am."

My father never read a book in his life, and it would be very hard to get a man like that to listen to an analyst who says "Let's discuss your problems." A man who says "I don't laugh" is not apt to go and say, "What's wrong with me?" or "Please help me to be a better person and richer in spirit." So many of those people who do need it just wouldn't benefit from it—they couldn't.

I think most people think that if you go and have a successful analysis or therapy, you don't have problems anymore. Well, you do but you just learn how, when they come up, not to let them get as bad as they were, not to let them take hold of you or take charge. You learn that at some point you've got to say, "Hey, wait, that's enough."

Why would I want to harm myself? Because I wanted to say to somebody else, "See how unhappy I am? It's all your fault." And you find out later that that's not the way to deal with it. I can't get back at somebody else by harming myself, because ultimately all I really do is harm myself. The other person is going to be harmed or not harmed according to what *his* life is like. I think that was one of the most significant things I learned. Most of the immature people I know would do things like this: they would refuse to be happy.

I don't think therapy is something everybody could really use. There are some very fortunate people in the world who don't have as many neurotic problems as other people. I came from a very neurotic background, what with our household and my parents. It was a very, very rough upbringing, and I paid for it later on. A lot of people don't come from that type of background. We can all use assistance once in a while when we don't know how to deal with certain problems, but I don't think everybody has to go through therapy.

Getting along with other people is just a by-product of getting along with yourself. For example, I *knew* my claustrophobia all existed inside of my mind. I would see other people on a plane reading newspapers and talking, so obviously it wasn't the surroundings that were at fault, but how I was dealing with them. So it's when you learn to deal with yourself that you can deal with the surroundings and the other people.

I would say most of my therapy was pleasurable. I mean, even when one would break down and start to cry, it was pleasurable, because it meant you were getting somewhere. I always felt I was in such good hands with Mildred. And I felt she was a human being rather than a robot. Many of the times she would just tell *me* stories. I mean, sometimes she spent half the session talking herself, and not even about me. But there was a point to her story, and I would learn something from it. So these sessions were exchanges rather than being very clinical. She just has a way of talking to people that says, "Listen, doesn't this make sense to you, what I'm saying?" This was her approach, rather than "Listen to me; what I have to say is for your own good."

Therapists were my disappointment in therapy. The only thing I would sometimes regret about the therapy itself was that it was time-consuming. It took a good two hours out of my day, and there were a lot of times when I really didn't want to go, because I would have to break up a whole day.

It was a big trip down to Mildred's office. Also, she had the worst elevator I ever saw, so I used to walk up the seven floors to her office; I mean, I would just not take a chance of being trapped on her elevator. So the worst thing about going to see her was the process of going to see her—but being there was great.

Just recently I was feeling very depressed, as I do every time I finish a project—we had just finished shooting this movie, *Murder By Death*. I always take a dip emotionally, because so much energy goes into the work, and then it ends. For a while I felt so bad I wished I could spend a lot of time speaking to Mildred, but, knowing I couldn't, I just flirted for a moment with the idea of finding a doctor out here. "Well, my brother was so and so; I met my mother when I was seven. . . ." I just wouldn't go through all that again. Mostly, though, I don't ever want to go through therapy again, because I don't want to be in that much trouble emotionally.

Adrienne Barbeau

In a rehearsal hall at Metromedia Square in Hollywood, Adrienne Barbeau sat silently while a director instructed her and her *Maude* co-stars, Bea Arthur and Bill Macy, on the way a scene was to be played later in the week before a live audience. When the group broke for lunch, Barbeau steered me into an adjacent room large enough for several hundred people but now occupied only by folding chairs stacked against a wall.

Dressed in a red tunic top of brushed terry cloth and a blue split skirt, the petite brunette was simultaneously businesslike and personable in her approach to the interview. An exuberant talker, she gave me an articulate and upbeat account of her experiences in therapy, recalling that they had begun when she was an unknown actress in New York and years away from success as Maude's daughter on the popular TV series.

In 1968 I was in New York in *Fiddler on the Roof,* playing one of the daughters. I had been in the show for about a year and a half and wanted to leave it but couldn't audition for another show. I was scared to death to audition. I'd buy the trade papers, take them home, read them and just put them away. And when I did audition I was so nervous I lost control of all my facial muscles. I'd stand across from an agent and shake.

I went to a good friend of mine, Peg Murray, who played the mother in *Fiddler*, and said I was thinking about going back into therapy. (I was in group therapy for about a year in 1966. I didn't have any money—I was trying to be an actress—and I had applied to St. Vincent's Hospital in New York because they had a low-cost program. But they didn't think I was in need of private therapy, so they put me in a group.)

Peg said something then that I thought was very valid. She said that, if nothing else, therapy would increase my earning power, because the more I knew about myself, the better off I'd be—especially in our industry.

Also, I started dating someone who had just begun in therapy, and he too suggested that I get into it. So I guess it was a combination of those things that sent me back into treatment.

I saw a woman, a psychologist, off and on for maybe two years. I realized that the last two or three times I had auditioned—prior to this inability to audition—I had come very, very close to getting roles that I wanted very badly, that would have been good for my career. And in each instance they had chosen another girl. So these were painful incidents and may have had something to do with the problem I was having after a year and a half in *Fiddler*.

The one area in which I've grown an enormous amount—because of therapy—is this: I feel better about myself. I know my value; I know my worth more. So if I walk in and audition and they say, "You're not right," I say, "OK, I'm not right," or "They didn't see it" (or whatever), but not, "Oh my God, I'm not right; I'm a terrible person." And basically that's what I was feeling in those years. My only value was through my talent, and if, God forbid, I was not talented, then I was not valuable. Now I can say I'm valuable as an individual whether or not I ever act again.

Therapy gave me a sense of myself, of who I was. I was a person at one time who would mirror anything I thought was wanted of me in order to be liked. If you had read a book and loved it and I read the book and hated it, I'd never say I hated it, because, God forbid, you wouldn't like me. Now I'm pretty much in touch with who I am and what I want, and I can ask for what I want and be myself without regard to the consequences. I'm not so worried that I won't be liked if I say what I'm thinking or feeling.

I was one of those teenagers or adolescents who never understood it when adults said teenagers have problems—because I was, I thought, super-healthy. I was a straight-A student, in student council, an actress and this and that. I was just sailing. I didn't think I had a problem in the world until I moved to New York, was on my own and faced the "real world"—for want of a better phrase.

And suddenly I saw patterns repeating themselves that I didn't like. They were patterns that weren't uncomfortable at that time but which I didn't want to be be repeating ten years from then. Like being attracted to men who weren't healthy, weren't available, weren't treating me well.

One of the things I realized about myself in therapy was that I had a very poor self-image. I just didn't think I was very valuable, and so I chose people who treated me as though I weren't very valuable. This poor self-image is not a very good personality trait, especially in the acting field, in which you've got to have some faith in myself.

The problem was that my parents were divorced when I was very young. I assume that part of what I experienced was feeling that if my father was leaving home, he was leaving *me*, and that was because I wasn't a nice person or had done something bad.

I can hardly remember anything about my childhood. I don't remember anything that happened before I was sixteen. I can only recall little bits and pieces—not the way most people I know can relate things from their childhood. I experienced my parents' divorce as my being abandoned, rejected. I also experienced having to be responsible for my mother and all that, but I was only twelve years old. I think at the time it was so painful that I just blocked it all out.

Anyway, as far as my relationships with men were concerned, what bothered me was my projection about what might happen if I continued along in the same manner. If I eventually wanted a home and children and security in a relationship—not necessarily marriage but an ongoing relationship—I found that the people who could offer those things were not attractive to me. And the people who were attractive to me were the ones who weren't going to stick around or offer any security or honesty. I was unable to be attracted to people who treated me well. What it really came down to, in fact, was that if a man treated me well, I'd wipe the floor with him.

After therapy I was able to have a relationship with a man who was stable and single and fairly healthy. That was a change already. Over the years I see the change, in that I'm attracted now to people who are healthier. Also, I've become much freer because I'm not so afraid of the response. My relationships with all people have changed in this way: I can say what I'm feeling.

I think my mother probably put a lot of emphasis on my having a career. She had me studying ballet when I was three years old and taking voice lessons when I was in the fifth grade. By the time I was sixteen I was in community theater in San José, and when I was eighteen I was entertaining troops overseas. I guess one of the things I dealt with in therapy was whether I was in this business for my mother or for me. Fortunately, I found out that I want to be here for myself as well as for her. I think if I had discovered that I didn't want to be here—that I was only here because of her—I would have been very resentful.

I think there is a danger of not being with the right therapist, and you don't know that until you try one or two. There were many times when my psychologist talked and I wouldn't understand. Her terminology was different from mine. In terms of therapy, that should have pointed out to me that if the communication wasn't great, I should have had the courage to say, "I don't understand." At least I realize I was blocked in that area. There were times when I should have said "I don't understand"—because I didn't.

I remember her being absolutely astonished when she asked, "What's the worst thing you can think of that could happen to you?" and I said, "Failing." She just couldn't believe that was the worst thing. I was very surprised to find out that not everybody was as terrified as I was of failing. I thought that was what everybody was worried about.

The only thing that caught me off-guard was if I would see my shrink late in the day and she fell asleep on me.

I almost had to learn to express anger. I was raised in a family in which it wasn't nice to get angry. Instead of getting angry, I would get hurt, turn it inside. If I had to act angry in a scene, I didn't know quite how to do it. So I was imitating. Even now it takes a lot to get me angry. But I do allow myself anger; I express it more.

I spent a year and a half in New York without dating anyone, and I learned from that that I can be alone and that I get along with myself, like myself and am strong.

I love finding out about myself, and I love seeing the changes. They're really exciting. I've wanted to give myself every chance to make relationships work, to make a job work—whatever.

I'd like to be able to take more chances to make an ass out of myself. In certain business situations I'm still afraid of appearing foolish, so I may not take a chance that would really open me up creatively.

The other thing I'd change is changing already—and it has to do with standing up for myself. I'm not good in dealing with money matters; I have an embarrassment about that. I have trouble asking for what I'm worth. It's not easy for me to negotiate or wheel and deal.

I know very few people who couldn't benefit from knowing more about themselves. In therapy a person has to want to change and to believe it is going to help him change.

Sid Caesar

Sid Caesar was slow to acknowledge my correspondence requesting an interview. I wrote several letters and made several calls before he admitted having heard from me and agreed to talk.

His wife of thirty-four years, Florence, met me at the door of their hilltop Beverly Hills house. Caesar himself appeared minutes later—in bedroom slippers and a plaid terry cloth robe—to greet me and then to excuse himself long enough to fetch a large stein of water.

As two maintenance men attended to the pool beyond the sliding glass doors behind us, Caesar recalled his decision, some twenty years earlier, to go into therapy. He was doing the *Show of Shows* then and was a man on top of the heap in television. Not long ago, I heard, he told a Los Angeles reporter that he had spent the intervening years "trying to get back on." His frustration in this area—which was mirrored in comments to me concerning the prevalence of "pap" in today's programming—is easy to understand. His comic talent, which many regard as bordering on genius, has been widely praised, and his fans are legion. Recently he has made a triumphant return to public view, notably in *Silent Movie* (the creation of his former TV writer, Mel Brooks) and *Fire Sale.*

A tall and powerful looking figure, Caesar spoke quietly, a tension underlying his words. Occasionally what he said took the form of a bit of *shtick* (as when he went through the standard questions of a talk-show host) and made me laugh. But the comedian himself never smiled.

I first went into therapy when I was doing the *Show of Shows*. I felt tense after doing a one-and-a-half-hour show live. Do you realize what that is? It's not just talking, talk-show style—where you sit down and ask, "Well, how you been, how you doing, oh what did you do then, oh what's your name, what's your real name, what's your daughter doing, do you have a dog, do you have a pigeon, do you have a cat?"—but doing entertainment that requires writing, rehearsal, sound effects, and so forth.

We were doing ninety minutes live with no cue cards and no laugh track. I was helping with the writing, doing a lot of the directing and then performing. And this was not just for twenty-two or twenty-four weeks a season but for thirty-nine weeks. After about ten weeks the strain became quite telling, so I wanted to know if I could get some relief. My medical doctor suggested a therapist.

When I first started out, I'd go five times a week, each for a forty-five-minute hour. There were times when I couldn't wait to get there to tell him a certain thing, but there were also times when I thought, "What am I going for?" And that's a good sign, because it means you're getting better. You become aware of the things that are happening around you and you start to ask questions.

You have times when you feel elated because the process is working and you're feeling good, and then all of a sudden you have a relapse. It's two steps forward and one step back. It's not straight up the hill and into the clouds and off into the wild blue yonder. And sometimes a lot of the results are latent. You understand a certain problem intellectually, but you don't *really* understand it. Later on you come up against the same problem, and you find that it doesn't bother you.

There are times when you find out things about yourself that are not too nice and other times when you find out things that you're really proud of. And sometimes you don't find out anything at all.

You think of your therapist as a father figure; you think that you want to hurt him; you think that you love him; you think that you don't need him or that you can't do without him. You go through every sort of feeling. That's normal.

As for dealing with the show, I learned to take it day to day. Sometimes you have a good show and feel happy and elated. Then, an hour and a half later, you say, "Well, wait a minute: I've got to do this again next week and try to do it better." You put your own strain on yourself; it's all from within.

When we went out on stage to do the *Show of Shows,* we were so full of adrenaline that if a sketch wasn't that great, we put extra energy into it to try to make it so. But that wasn't much consolation if it didn't go.

At that time I didn't realize how well much of it was turning out, because I was so preoccupied with other things that were happening around me. When you're in the middle of the forest, you can't see the trees.

One of the things that drove me was the feeling that everything had to be *right now—everything.* I got used to operating this way because, when I was doing the show, everything *had* to be done right then. There was a need for immediacy. I took the show home with me—which you shouldn't do—and let it be all-consuming. In analysis you find that it doesn't have to be that way, that it's better if you think things over and plan your strategy. The main thing was to realize you can't conquer the world in a minute. You can't do it. It takes time.

When you're young, you want to do it right and the best that you can. But sometimes things don't work out just right and you blame yourself for it. But now I understand, and I don't blame anybody; I don't even blame myself. I say, "Well, that's the way the world is today." It's a different world: pablum is in. And it's going to get more and more watery.

My therapy also involved my talking about my reaction to people, which I used in the show. When you take on a show for an hour and a half, where are you going to draw all your material from? Life! So I became a little more astute in watching people, seeing how they did things and what kinds of mannerisms they had.

You find out an awful lot of things about yourself and an awful lot of things about different apprehensions that were really unnecessary. You didn't have to have the apprehensions; you didn't have to be afraid. You turn on the light and see the table and then you don't have to walk into it anymore, which is being masochistic and hurting yourself. Life is hard enough without it.

You mustn't get carried away with yourself. The most you can be is a human being. That's the top you can be, to feel for your fellow man.

And you have to learn to live with yourself. Not everything that happens in life is going to make you feel good: certain things make you feel a little down. So you take them in stride. Don't pester yourself too much, don't get angry with yourself, because that's how you do the most harm.

My first analyst worked out well, but after about five years he had to leave, to do some research work for a college. The second one, whom I didn't like, I got rid of right away. He was mainly interested in writing books and being Mr. Psychiatrist of the World. "You want to make money, I've got a good deal for you." *That* he responded to. He didn't deal in human beings, just books, money and making a name for himself—and that I didn't need. I said, "You be a big man on somebody else's time and money." The third man I went to helped me an awful lot.

Generally speaking, there were no revelations. No clouds parted; nothing came down out of the sky. Slowly you find out that you're not the center of the universe, that there are other people in the world and they have just as much right to the world as you or anybody else.

I'm kind of a solitary person. I don't make fun unless I'm on stage: for me, it's a business. I like to read history and, of all things, physics. And in doing this, I find a great relief, a great outlet. When you start to get into physics, you find out how small everything is—and how big everything is, from the microism to the macroism. It changes your perspective a lot.

Once or twice a year I see a therapist here in L.A. I check on myself just to make sure I'm OK, because you *can* go back to your old habits. Like why dwell on something that is disturbing when there's nothing you can really do until you can get on the phone the next day? Why let it disturb your night's sleep? You'll do something about it when you get up in the morning. And then you *do* it—that relieves it right away.

Before therapy, I wouldn't feel happy about things. You feel guilty because you feel you're not worthy. So instead of just taking things in stride—and saying "I worked very hard for this"—you feel bad. Now, finally, I have found the ability to enjoy it when something good happens—and that takes a lot of learning.

Bruce Dern

Bruce Dern was late. His secretary and I waited for him in a Beverly Hills apartment lent to us by an assistant director on the actor's last movie. Speculation that he might be having a problem finding the address ended with the sound of his Jeep truck pulling up at the curb.

Sockless in sneakers, wearing old blue jeans and a jeans-style shirt, Dern looked as though he might have been on the way to the set of one of the bike films he made early in his career. Tall and wiry, he runs several miles each day, eschews alcohol and drugs, and seems accordingly fit and youthful at age forty.

His eye-catching secretary, whom he identified as one of his closest friends, busied herself in the kitchen, occasionally bringing in drinks. He kidded that he might adopt her if she weren't already over twenty-one and no longer deductible.

The first man ever to kill John Wayne on screen (in *The Cowboys*), Dern was also in *The Great Gatsby, Smile, Family Plot* and another movie in which the star was—literally—a dog (*Won Ton Ton*). When we spoke he had finished work on *Black Sunday,* a film to which he referred frequently and enthusiastically ("the best work I've ever done"), and was eagerly anticipating its release.

His talk was fast-paced and engaging, liberally sprinkled with expletives which helped convey his intensity and which at times provoked laughter, even from Dern himself.

I think most people go into therapy because they feel they're having trouble communicating their real thoughts and feelings under pressure, or at any time at all. They go because they need a friend, and they feel that an analyst is a friend. There is no one in their life they can be as intimate with verbally as they would like. So they go to a psychiatrist because they feel they can trust him with things they can trust nobody else with.

I went to an analyst because I was having trouble in my second marriage. I was having problems in that I was running around on my wife. My wife said, "You're a sick motherfucker and you'd better go." So I went, and I found out I had problems, but I wasn't *that* sick.

First I went to a guy named Philip Oderberg, who was a psychologist. But in 1966 SAG [Screen Actors Guild] did not give you any money toward going to a psychologist—only a psychiatrist. So, although Oderberg was a very helpful guy, I had to quit going to him because I didn't have the money.

Next, my wife and I went to a man here in Beverly Hills named Norman Trabulus, who was also very good. After six months Trabulus said "You two people should not be together," so we're not together anymore: we got a divorce.

When I met my present wife, Andrea, who was in my acting class, I spent about a week with her and then had my next appointment with Dr. Trabulus. I told him about her, said I wasn't running around with whores a whole lot anymore—I had done that quite a bit—and would like to spend the rest of my life with Andrea. I also told him I didn't need to come see him anymore, and he said, "I think you're right." That was eight years ago, and I've never been back since, or felt the need for it.

But I learned things in therapy. I found out that I didn't really love the girl I was married to. We'd had a little girl who had drowned in a swimming pool about five years earlier. That was a hard thing on our marriage, which had been in trouble anyway. We just didn't like each other.

My wife was a good girl, but she was just not for me and I was not good for her. She didn't realize this: she was trying to live out the Paul Newman–Joanne Woodward dream, and it would just never work that way.

At any rate, I should never have had the kid. I'm just not a responsible parent. I don't mean that's why the child died, because it isn't. She was with a nurse who went to answer the phone and left her by the pool. Then the nurse looked all around the house—everywhere but the pool—and when she finally looked in the pool, it was too late.

My ex-wife and I then had another daughter, who is now nine. As soon as we saw the child was going to make it out of the hospital and all, the marriage really started coming apart. Our new daughter was almost like a guilt child. I mean, my wife and I both had this terrible feeling, and maybe we stayed together because God had shown us something. My ex-wife was Catholic, and she believed a lot of things like that. I didn't know what I believed. I knew neither one of us was responsible for the child's death, but, at the same time, we had hired the girl [nurse], and the girl was a moron.

I'm a Method actor, and there is an exercise in Method acting called emotional memory. The key to it is taking some event that has happened in your life and remembering the sensual things that were going on that day. Now in *Black Sunday* there were two scenes where I had to go to pieces. For both scenes I used the same emotional memory. The difference was that one was this terrible guilt feeling I have about the kid's death, which leads me to one kind of emotional response. The other was being left alone to deal with it, which brings me another kind of emotional response. When I got back to the house following the kid's death, I had to go through the first hour and a half by myself: my wife wasn't there. And then I left my wife about a year later, and for three months I had to go through it alone.

In therapy I found out that I had a lot of confidence, but I had no confidence in myself as a coming factor in the motion picture industry. And the doctors made me aware—particularly Dr. Trabulus—that I could be a driving force in this industry; that, as an actor, I had genius proportions and great talent and that I shouldn't despair that it was never going to happen for me. Now, ten years later, it turns out they were right. I mean, I'm a movie star—not to myself but to the two hundred people here in Beverly Hills. Every time they make up a list now, I'm on the list. All this list shit is terrifying, because everybody's list is different. I fought twenty years to get on a list and to be approvable.

I learned why I rode motorcycles. I never rode a motorcycle until I started doing the bike films and got an image of a bad guy. And I enjoyed it because I had never been a bad guy. When I was in high school I was a pussy. I was afraid of bad guys. In Winnetka the guys who rode motorcycles were always leaving school and going to Texas in the middle of the year. They didn't give a shit. They weren't athletes or anything, but they were neat guys. I mean, we all had our idols in high school, and I looked up to guys like that.

My whole life has been based upon my pursuit to be an artist as an actor; my hobby has been running, and my general day-to-day thing is working on relationships with people because I never worked on any the first twenty years of my life.

The friends I made through the eighth grade were all taken away from me very rudely when I was made to go away to prep school. I had New Trier High School to go to—the finest public high school in the world—and my parents sent me to Choate, with five hundred of the unhappiest kids I ever saw in my life. Why? I was playing with the wrong kinds of kids: I was gambling, playing cards and betting on football and baseball games. But I wasn't into sexual things, I wasn't drinking, I wasn't into dope, and I wasn't making it with another guy. We didn't even know what sex was until I was a sophomore in high school.

Anyway, I belonged at New Trier. I got to come back my last two years [of high school], but that was the cruelest thing of all. I couldn't tell the guys that my parents had sent me to prep school because I was playing with *them*; I had to tell them that I wanted to try prep school. So I had to cover the whole thing for my parents.

Well, as soon as I told them I had wanted to try prep school, they said, "We're not good enough for you? New Trier's not good enough for you? Well, kiss off, you asshole." That was very tough on me.

I've always found it easier to deal with women. I've always related to women much better. I think most of the guys I know of who have attained the level of success I have deal with women much better and more often than with men. I would say Redford is the only guy who doesn't. But Nicholson and Beatty certainly do. Their pursuits are in that area more. And guys threaten them; it's a sense of competition.

With me, it's just that there weren't too many guys who gave a shit about me. Maybe it was always a throwback to coming back to New Trier in second place and right away having relationships with girls that were really about as bizarre as anything you can imagine.

I mean, I was searching for a friend, not a fuck-mate. I went steady with a girl for my whole senior year and never even touched her breasts—while everybody else was getting laid. And I'd drive a hundred and twenty miles to fuck a whore rather than mess around with this girl. I felt I loved her—I kissed her with meaning and all that stuff—but I was just not into horniness at that level in high school—I took care of that in another way.

There was a barrier that came up between my family and me—because of those two years at Choate—that was never broken down. And from the time I was nine years old on, I was also sent away to camp every summer.

When I was sent away, I obviously felt that I was alone. So in later life, when I did leave the house, I didn't want to have to experience things alone. I realized that in those years and summers I had experienced a lot of things, but I had no pal to experience them with.

I never had a sit-down, one-to-one conversation with my father in my life until about a year before he died (when I was twenty). So that was being alone, and that was very rough on me.

When I talked to the analysts I realized that the emotional things that I talked to them about were not the kid's death and things like that but the fact that the house man took me to the fucking train all the time when I had to go away to camp and prep school. My parents never got up early in the morning to meet me. They didn't give a shit. Those are the things that bothered me most and gave me the most hostility toward my family.

I thought therapy would be much heavier than it was, only because of hearsay. I kept thinking I'd lie down on the couch and be sucking my thumb, tears rolling out of my eyes, saying that I wanted to fuck my mom in the ass. But I found out that I don't want to punch mom and I don't want to fuck her. Does this mean I'm not normal? I thought some big traumatic things were gonna happen: that I was gonna twitch or go into some kind of thing, but I didn't.

And I thought maybe I would get much more emotional than I did. All the therapists with me were conversationalists and friends. But I felt I was kinda "doing sentence" to be there with them, and they got that outta me right away, at the beginning. I was told, honest to God, that I was not a real deep case of needing therapy—I'm sure everybody says that. They said you can use a period of time with us talking together, but you should not become an addict. Because it can become a dependency that's unbelievable.

A big thing I got out of therapy was the ability to make a decision and follow it through. Before I went to them I could make a decision and follow it through but would have enormous guilt about what I had done (more concerning relationships than anything else). Now I just do it and carry it out.

I feel one of the problems with people who go to therapists is that there's not enough "shopping" done. I hate to use that word—I'm sure therapists would just kick my teeth in for that—but it can't be that one guy is right for everybody. I think too often we just go and there we are.

Therapy was enormously expensive, and that was a disappointment. I was teaching acting at the time, and I was giving it away to most of the students because they believed in me—I was almost like a messiah to them. So when I went to the analyst I thought, "Gee, why is he charging me so much?" I just thought it would be nice if it didn't cost quite so much; if you could have the feeling that they were more interested really in you than the dollars and cents. I think what people get turned off by a lot sometimes is the expense of it. It just staggers them. They hear the clock ticking and they feel they don't get a show-me value out of it.

Most of us dislike ourselves because we feel that we think things that we shouldn't think. I mean, I was into pornography fifteen years ago—not making it but watching it—and everybody used to say, "Oh, man, that's sick." And I said, "Will I grow hair?" I talked to the doctors about it, about when I went to whores and everything. And whores weren't fulfilling for me; they were just an outlet. Better to pay a whore and get it over with than knock up a girl in the acting class and take advantage of somebody because I was a teacher or actor and they were not. So I got to like myself better [through therapy] because I came to terms with myself.

I've never been a jealous person. I mean, I'm jealous of Jack Nicholson, getting every part in the world and me only getting half of them. I mean, I'd like to have the opportunity to have my pick of roles like he does, and I haven't quite got that yet. So I'm jealous in that way. But I'm not jealous about my wife fucking a young guy, and I never have been in any one of the three marriages. If they want to go out and have an affair, that's fine. I've just never been possessive of somebody else's body or spirit: I don't believe in that, and I don't want a woman to be possessive of me in that way. One of the reasons Andrea and I get along is that she feels the same way.

I think the greatest catastrophe in the American marital state has to do with this sort of thing. When I went to France to do this movie, *The Twist*, for Claude Chabrol, I realized the French don't look at things the way we do. I mean, they've all got mistresses; they've got so many people you gotta have a program to know who's with whom. But that's not true here. Here, it's this divine kind of house of marriage, and within that house, fidelity is the first thing the marriage is based on. Well, that's horseshit, because sex is an animalistic thing at times.

Sex has never been a thing to get jealous about. I wouldn't want to come home and find Andrea lying on the floor for six hours kissing a guy on the mouth and telling him how much she loved him. But if I came home and found the same guy fucking her, it wouldn't bother me—as much. I mean, I wouldn't want to come home and *see* it, and I don't want to be *told* about it, but if she wants to carry on and say, "Well, something's going on, but it doesn't mean anything, it's just sexual," *fine*.

I'm finding out every day things that touch me and things that don't touch me as an artist—and I just keep filing them away. I get very depressed sometimes out of jealousy—and this is terrible to admit—when guys I don't believe deserve better breaks in their career than I've gotten to date get in movies that get great reviews and do great business and are *crap*. I go apeshit.

And there are times when I'm happy for somebody getting a bad review. . . . There is no justice in art. Maybe that's why I hang on to running so much, because the watch doesn't lie. You go from here to there in whatever time it takes you. It's a purist sport. You don't need somebody else. You're really competing against yourself.

One of the big emotions I have to deal with still is that at forty years old I get tremendously nervous before these races that I run because I want to do what I'm capable of doing. And I want to be able to do what I'm capable of doing as an artist. It's maddening to have agents and producers say, "Yeh, well, he's maybe the best actor in the business, but he's not Clint Eastwood, and he never will be." That throws you into a depression more than anything else; that's the thing that hurts. I don't want to be Clint Eastwood. I want to play interesting multidimensional people in movies that are entertaining. That's all I've ever wanted out of it.

I think my talent will always keep me where I've gotten to now, but it would be nice to be in one big hit simply because then I would get some roles that I'm not getting a chance at now.

When I went into therapy I wanted to be freer as a talker . . . I couldn't have had this conversation ten years ago. I consented to it because I feel there is a definite correlation between the Method actor and analysis. I feel the true Method actor—the person who has an instrument and is able to play it well and fully according to the role—is a person who has had some kind of psychiatric experience with himself or through the aid of a doctor.

I don't feel that I would be where I am as an actor today had I not had the psychiatric experience I had, even though it was just about a year in total. To me, art can only begin if you are aware of yourself.

Shelley Winters

"I live on the wrong side of the tracks, honey," Shelley Winters quipped on the phone, taking care to provide me with precise directions for finding her apartment, which turned out to be the entire ground floor of an older Spanish-style building in Beverly Hills.

On my first visit, the Academy Award–winning actress was in the throes of a bad cold. Wearing a nightgown and a robe, she exchanged greetings with me and then stretched out on her living room couch, where her maid covered her with a blanket. Somehow it was like a scene right out of a Shelley Winters film.

Our interview was interrupted intermittently by the ringing of one or the other of two phones which Winters had placed on the floor by the couch. One call had her talking to a foreign filmmaker in an odd mix of English and broken Italian.

A framed poster from *A Place in the Sun* (in which she co-starred with Elizabeth Taylor and Montgomery Clift) and a bound script on the coffee table were the only hints at the life work of the apartment's owner, whose career on stage and screen has been long and distinguished.

"Up to about ten years ago, people were very secretive about going to psychiatrists," said Shelley Winters, who often alludes—fleetingly—to her involvement in analysis on talk shows that are seen by millions. But the prospect of actually detailing her experiences in treatment at first gave her pause. And indeed, after our first meeting she had second thoughts about what she had told me—"grave reservations," as she put it. But during a second conference she decided to allow our interview to run intact, and in fact only expanded on her previous comments.

I've been in and out of analysis for about twenty years, with two different doctors. In 1954 I had been conditioned, like every other woman in this country (if not the world), to be what the Italians call a "sex bomb." That was the only thing that would turn a man on to you, as a woman and an actress. You sort of hid your intellect and got by on cunning, presenting this sort of "blonde bombshell" image.

If you have to be *the* most beautiful and *the* sexiest, then your feelings of insufficiency are multiplied. You have this sort of visual and personality thing that is put on you, and then you have to maintain it all the time publicly, while forever trying to escape from it in private life. I think this is what happened to Marilyn Monroe, and she wasn't fortunate enough, as she got older, to depend on her natural comedic talents and wit to "grow older."

So I was very dissatisfied with my career and my life. I had made an awful lot of pictures when I was under contract. I would do one good picture for every six lousy ones.

I reached a point emotionally where I felt I needed help, and Arthur Laurents suggested Dr. Judd Marmor. I went to him for about a year, and I think I mostly told him jokes. Anything that was painful I would make jokes about.

I would be fifteen minutes late for every appointment, then have an appointment afterwards so that I would have to leave five minutes early. The fifty minutes got reduced to thirty minutes of jokes.

After I had been with him for a year, he became discouraged with my progress. And I looked around and realized that when I had a good director, I thought I was a very good actress—but when I didn't, I didn't think I was very good. So I decided to move to New York.

When I told Judd of my decision and discussed it with him, he suggested I see a woman therapist in New York.

Up to then I had been a kind of Hollywood sex kitten, not on the level that Marilyn Monroe and Brigitte Bardot achieved, but rather in a minor way. But during that time I still managed to make some distinguished films, like *A Double Life, A Place in the Sun, Night of the Hunter* and *The Big Knife.*

So when I got an offer to do the play *A Hatful of Rain* in New York, I moved myself, my child and my mother there. The play opened and it was a hit.

During its run I went through a considerable amount of tough analysis, which made me see the truth of the process of psychiatry. I saw the results in the way I handled myself in that play. But then I came back out to California. I married Tony Franciosa. (The sex image again.) My doctor said that if she had had the power, she would have institutionalized me to prevent that marriage.

In a funny kind of way, if your sexy movie image is what a man is attracted to and you must respond to him, he doesn't want to see the other, the real person. The image is what he likes. This happened to Marilyn often, and it also happened to me a couple of times. (I saw Marilyn—when she was all dressed to go out, made up and looking gorgeous—take it all off and start all over again because she had to present this mask to the world. And it wasn't really her.) It's one of the occupational hazards.

It's very hard for two actors to have a permanent relationship. You have to say, "Do I want a successful career, or am I going to risk that for a marriage?" And if you don't know if the marriage is going to work out, you're going to opt for the career.

When someone goes out with you on the first two or three dates, it seems funny when people come up and ask you for your autograph right when you may be in the middle of the most intimate and personal type of conversation. They barge right in. You have to be polite: you can't say "Get lost" or something. The first time it's only annoying, but the third or fourth time your date's ego goes on the line, and then it's all over.

I think when I went to my doctor first I envisioned that when I got the analysis, I would walk into the sunset with a handsome man, with his hand in mine. An actor perhaps. But the reality is that it can't happen this way. An actor's work will take him all over the world, and he'll want somebody—not an actress—who will be able to be at his beck and call.

Naturally most men want their own careers and their own glory, so it's a difficult arrangement if you're an actress. And there's nothing in analysis that fixes that situation. You just learn to handle it better. I just see it more clearly now, so I don't take it as a personal failure on my part that I'm not able to make that kind of life arrangement. I could have done what Joanne Woodward did, which was to abandon her career in favor of her marriage. She used to work only where and when her husband was working. But I would never be happy doing that.

Anyway, my marriage to Tony Franciosa was an unhappy one, so I stayed in California for two or three years and then went back to New York again after the divorce.

I didn't go back into therapy at first, because I felt that I was cured. Everything was fine, I thought, and I didn't need it. But things happened which made me see that I did.

You don't eliminate problems by fixing them on top, or just getting rid of symptoms. Unless you deal with the feelings you had as a child, they affect how you function as an adult.

As a child, I had a sort of imaginary world that I escaped into. I used to walk all over Brooklyn and pretend and make-believe and imagine. I was very frightened. I couldn't protect myself against the real problems of my ghetto life, so I protected myself against imaginary problems. I would shift it all over into that area.

This stands me in good stead as an actress, because I can imagine myself very strongly into any given situation. When I've had to play roles which were kind of strange, I could pick out a specific experience I had as a child and magnify it into what I needed in my work.

It's funny, because when I first went into analysis, I thought I'd had a very happy childhood, a wonderful mother and father, and everything was hunky-dory. But I was a Depression baby, and we had a very rough time. If anything, I had to run before I knew how to walk. That makes you bowlegged emotionally.

One of the things was the fact that my mother had to work, my father was away, and I would be alone. I would come home from school at three, cook dinner, clean up the house, and be all alone until ten o'clock at night when my mother came home.

We were never hungry, my mother and father did love me, and my mother was very proud of my abilities and pushed me in the direction I wanted to go. But there were periods that were very tough, especially for a youngster. I had just come from St. Louis to New York, from a suburb to a big, crowded ghetto. I remember sitting on a bench on the street, counting the cars and saying to myself, "When the eighteenth one goes by"—or the hundredth—"my mother will come home."

There I was, a kid eleven years old, having to clean a house, shop, cook, and be alone for long periods. In a way, the childhood that I should have had I never quite had. I think when I was thirty-five I tried to go back and get it.

I think people who are attracted to theater are inclined to need love and reach for love and want the love of that audience. I mean, *nobody* can compete with the praise of fifteen hundred people applauding and yelling "Bravo." The ones who go for that are the ones who lack love.

I started going to this woman analyst, Dr. Viola Bernard, in New York in 1956, and I guess I've had about a hundred sessions with her. My work made it very convenient to leave town any time we got near something that was too painful. There were pictures I could have skipped—rather than skipping my analysis—but they provided a good excuse to run away. Some, though, were very illustrious films that I should have done—and legitimate reasons for my leaving.

All my appointments with my doctor in New York were for late in the day, so if I didn't show up, she wasn't cheating somebody else out of a session. But now I'm on time, and when I make an appointment, I keep it.

When I began my analysis in New York, my analyst said, "You'll spend the next few years fighting against me so you don't have to face certain things you deplore."

Once I ran out of my analyst's office, ran to the airport and took a plane to California—with no luggage. Usually a good therapist knows when to coddle you and when to be very firm.

Sometimes you're reacting as you did when you were a child, and they have to treat you like a child.

You spend about a year trying to seek their approval. For instance, I didn't want to talk to her while I was very depressed, although doctors prefer seeing you during your bad times, because they can learn more about your "acting out" of problems. The doctor finally says to you, "Look, it doesn't matter whether I like you or not. Just use my knowledge."

For the longest time I would never discuss my work. I felt my talent was inspirational, and if I talked about it, it would go away.

I used to be very superstitious. And instead of really believing in my own talent and ability, I thought it was luck. So I let myself be used when I was under contract, by presenting an image of myself that today's young actresses wouldn't allow. They're intelligent women, and they won't let themselves be sold to the public in just any fashion the studio sees fit.

I've never come to terms yet with the fact that I'm overweight. I think that if I couldn't get a job for six months or a year because of weight, I would get thin. But unfortunately I get parts for which they want me to be heavier. And I think that's a mistake for me, and I'm not reconciled to that.

I think I'm very confusing to the public. First they see me in films and then they see me on talk shows. I've had fans who have written me asking, "Who is the real Shelley Winters?" They see the sort of nonsense role I play sometimes and then they see the real me on talk shows. They don't know who's who, which is which. But of course, as an actress, you have different roles in which you play different people.

My problems are reframed now. I understand that there are solutions for some problems and no solutions for others. For example, I know many actresses who get their faces lifted and fight a constant battle against the aging process. But I think this is very sad. One of the realities I've learned is that, with luck and health, you get older. That reality we must all face.

I have many girl friends who don't work anymore, who can't work. And there are some who won't play mothers or similar roles which require that they appear as older women. A twenty-five year-old girl should be played by someone that age and not a forty-year-old who is trying to look twenty-five. In every picture there's one part for a twenty-five-year-old girl, but there are many other parts, too.

This is an area in which I think women's lib is going to be helpful to women. In our society it's almost as if older men are acceptable but older women aren't. It's as if when a woman is over forty she should disappear. This is a situation in our society that's very evil.

I don't go to my analyst on a very regular basis anymore. If I'm in New York I might have four or five sessions over a four- or five-month period. If I don't think something is going exactly right, in my personal life or my work, I may call her. We're sort of friends now.

People go into therapy when they're very unhappy and perhaps have a glimmer that they're not living up to their potential of happiness or fulfillment in work or life. Going into therapy is a sign of health, because a person is recognizing that he needs help.

It's very hard to be a mature, normal, well-balanced person. I think the outside pressures are so bad now that a goodly percentage of our population needs help in one form or another. Therapy doesn't promise you that you'll go into the sunset with everything roses, but I think it helps you deal in a more constructive way with what happens to you in this world.

I know one of the reasons I've had such a long career is my analysis. When people ask, "What the hell has your psychiatry done for you?" I have to say "I'm *here,* whereas a lot of my contemporaries are not. I have a lot of longtime friends. I still have a marvelous career. I have a lovely daughter, two beautiful apartments on both coasts, and I travel all over the world. I have all kinds of experiences and meet all kinds of people—and, for the most part, I deal well with them. You can't have everything, but I've got a lot."

Tony Randall

"I'm *so* embarrassed," Tony Randall said plaintively, as he arrived at L.A.'s Shubert Theatre forty minutes late for our second interview. "I who am never late, I who pride myself on a perfect memory. I didn't forget, you know. I really don't want to talk about my analysis. That's how I let this happen."

With that bit of self-analysis out of the way, the slight, still boyish looking star of *The Odd Couple* (in which he was then appearing on stage) and *The Tony Randall Show* ushered me into his sparsely furnished dressing room, where he would prepare for the day's matinee performance.

As he changed from his casual street clothes to the button-down shirt, tie and blue blazer he would wear in the play, he girthed himself with a cloth contraption designed to ease the back pain with which he is sporadically plagued.

"I don't think my case will take up much space in your book," he told me, dismissing his story as not being "dramatic" enough. But, exuberant and articulate, Randall opened up about himself in a way he rarely does. When a PR man stopped by and asked if our interview was something he should know about, Randall sent him scurrying off; he obviously did not want any interference.

Then, applying his makeup as we talked, Randall plowed his way through a free-form conversation punctuated both by laughter and occasional expressions of painful remembrance.

I'm certain most people go into therapy because they're desperate. They don't go until it's almost too late. They do it to avoid suicide. And I suppose that's what a great many people never understand: that the great value of treatment is not that it ever cures you but that it prevents suicide.

Years ago, I told a girl I knew that I was having terrible problems and knew I needed help. She recommended that I see Dr. Paul Hoch, who was the head of some psychiatric services for the whole state of New York. So I called him up and had a conference with him, and he said, "Vell, you have many fears." And he assigned me to one of his students who was just beginning to practice.

I don't think I would have killed myself back then [without therapy]; I think I just would slowly have disintegrated. I couldn't handle my problems; they were too much for me. I did think about suicide a lot, but I don't think I would have got to the point of doing it. I just probably would have slogged on under this terrible burden that I couldn't hold.

Most people don't want to admit they need therapy, although the fact is that everyone on earth needs it, just as everyone needs to go to the dentist and everyone needs to have his eyes checked every two years.

That's easily proved when you consider how many automobile accidents we have every year. Consider how perfectly rational people become irrational when they're placed behind a wheel. Just that much power at their disposal—and you'll forgive the Freudian insight if I say that it's coming out from between their legs—makes them a little bit irrational—and dangerous.

There are very many standard manifestations that something's wrong with you, that you have emotional problems. The most common ones are claustrophobia, insomnia, impotence, frigidity, extreme forgetfulness, the inability to make a decision and, above all, the inability to fall in love. Feelings of helplessness are another indication that a person may need help, as are irrational fears of almost anything.

I knew one woman who was petrified of bees. She couldn't be anywhere except closed up in her house because she was certain bees were everywhere. That's not crazy: there *are* bees everywhere, and she probably *had* been stung, but most of us don't worry about it all the time.

The form that your manifestation takes is meaningless. It's just that you're full of fear and you can't live that way. So the mind has a trick called encapsulization. All your fears are directed toward some subject—in my friend's case, bees—so you're able to function in the rest of your life. Otherwise you'd be paralyzed totally by fear.

I knew a man, a big executive at CBS, who went around nauseated for several years. He was on the verge of vomiting all the time, and he *did* vomit frequently. Can you imagine living that way? The agony of it! Any second he felt his food might be coming back up. He went through therapy and told me all about it.

Ulcers are another extreme example of people just being torn apart by emotions on the inside. You are just turning them against yourself.

The most terrible symptom I had was insomnia. You know how awful it is to go one night without sleep, but imagine going six hundred nights! I'll tell you how it came about—and I think around seven million other men had the same experience I did. I'd never had a sleepless night in my whole life. I was in the army four years, and the day I learned I was going to be discharged, that night I didn't sleep, and then I didn't sleep for two years. That sudden fear of being on my own was the thing. The army was a great mother, a great womb. Every decision was made for you: today you'll wear your o-d's [olive drabs], this afternoon at two you'll change to your fatigues, here's your food, here's your salary, here's the doctor. Everything was done for you. Suddenly you're going to be expelled and be absolutely on your own, have to earn a living and make every decision for yourself. It threw people.

I felt my therapy was a positive thing all along. It's all so illusory in some ways, because after the first session I was able to sleep. You think "I'm cured"—and that's why it's so easy for quacks to function, because symptoms are often very easily cured. But to get at the causes is very difficult.

My shrink was very easy to take. He had developed the art of listening sympathetically and saying almost nothing, just nodding, seeming to be friendly, listening. And that *is* an art.

I remember having one extremely erotic dream about him, in which I made him a woman. There I suddenly realized "He's a woman," and I got extremely horny about him in my sleep. I put long hair on him, and although he was in fact chubby, I made him a nice zaftig, big-bosomed woman, and I was all over him. I had a lot of difficulty telling him that the next session. He didn't want to go into it too deeply, I don't think. But we were honest about it.

I frequently was late for sessions; I who am *never* late, always early, I would be late for sessions. They were painful, of course; it *is* painful. And then there are sessions when you cannot think of a thing to say; you simply are blocked, like a writer sitting at a typewriter.That's when it's very good to talk about dreams, because he can always say, "What did you dream last night?" and you start dredging up a dream. Or he can say, "That dream we talked about two weeks ago: tell me that one again." That's always an interesting thing to do, because you'll tell it differently; you'll remember it differently.

It was in a dream that I discovered the true nature of my relationship with my father. I dreamed of my uncle, one I loved very much, and I was a little boy sitting on his lap just hugging him and kissing him and loving him. I woke up thinking how much I missed him—he was dead by then—and how much I had always loved him. The next day I sat talking with the analyst about that, and as I talked I realized it *wasn't* Uncle Jessie, it was my father. It dawned on me that I loved him. I had always thought I hated him. That night I called my sister and said, "I always thought I hated daddy, but I didn't; I loved him. *He* hated *me*." And she said, "Oh, I could have told you that years ago."

We were strangers, my father and I. He was too old: that was the main problem. My father was about sixty when I was born, and he just didn't have the patience to sit with a child and play with him. He had been a bachelor all his life, and he just couldn't adjust. It wasn't his fault really; he was a good man. But it might just as well have been the postman or a policeman on the beat—just someone I didn't know.

As we grew older it got worse, and we became cold; not merely strangers but cold, distant, icy strangers. He disapproved of me entirely all my life; he *always* disapproved of me.

For a long time I was so ashamed of being in therapy that I couldn't talk about it. I didn't tell it to a soul. I didn't even tell my wife. Then one day I told her and—big deal, who cares? In my circle, there was a euphemism for going to the analyst: it was called going to the dentist. And everybody I knew went to the dentist. I used to play ball with a guy every day, five days a week, and he'd always say, "We've gotta play in a hurry today because I have to get to the dentist." And I didn't understand how anyone could have his teeth worked on all the time. One day I said, "You poor fellow, is it root canal work?" And he said "no" and then told me what he really meant.

There's an even better story, about a certain acting teacher—generally regarded as the best—who had a talented student who was so nervous he couldn't get up and act. He'd begin to literally tremble before the class. Anyway, this kid went to the teacher and asked if he could help him get a job in summer stock. So this teacher said to him, "I don't think you're ready to work. I think you need a dentist." So this kid came back in the fall and showed him his teeth. He had spent the entire summer and thirty-five hundred dollars having all his teeth capped. That's a true story.

The main thing you learn through therapy is to live with yourself, to accept yourself. The typical neurotic hates himself—or has a very low opinion of himself, in any case. He thinks everything is wrong with him and that if he were really an OK guy, he wouldn't have such contemptible failings. In therapy you learn that your failings aren't comtemptible, they're only human. You learn to forgive yourself and to live with yourself. And you learn another thing: that you're never going to get over your failings. I remember saying to my therapist, "Why am I *like* that?" And he said, "Because you're built that way." Now that sounds like advice anybody could give you, but this is technical and deep and results from much analysis of all the evidence and data you've presented to him. People *are* built different ways; certain things are just built in, and you're not going to change them. But you modify them, and, above all, you modify your relationship to them; you learn to live with yourself and to like yourself and accept yourself. You see, the person who can't accept himself never can accept anyone else.

The most difficult thing for me to accept about myself is that I'm a nervous wreck, that I have a terrible need to prove myself all the time. It gets a little personal and embarrassing, but the failings people have don't mean that life is finished; you get another chance and you try again. I guess it's the way a good businessman or a good gambler learns to operate: today I lost, but tomorrow I'll win. But that was always my feeling about *anything*, that if I lost, that was the end; I was finished. If I tried to hang a picture on the wall and I didn't hang it right and the plaster broke, I'd think, "I'm through, I'm no good, I might as well jump out the window." I'd just go into the depths of despair over anything. Anything seemed the end. You learn to live with your daily failures. Tomorrow you'll do better.

You learn that creativity has nothing to do with therapy. Many people think they must be creative because they're neurotic. I'll tell you a peculiar thing about homosexuality. If you see a ballet company in America, you can see that all the men are homosexual, or half of them. But if you see the Russian ballet, it's clear that they're not: they're very male men. But why is that? Well, my analysis is that we still in this country have this anti-intellectual bias about the arts and the peculiar, stupid and irrational view that the arts are really an effeminate thing, not for real men. The result is that if a man is effeminate, he presumes he must have talent. So homosexual men go into the arts with no other reason, no other justification than that they are homosexual.

The fact that they've proved that many great men were neurotic doesn't mean a thing. Most of the human race is neurotic in one way or another. The fact is that this thing called genius has been visited upon every conceivable type of man, from the craziest to the most bland and dull. Mozart, in his ordinary life, was the dullest little man. You read his letters home to his sister and father and they betray the most ordinary little mind. Nothing at all special. But when he sat down to write music, he was the greatest genius God has yet made. So you can't make any conclusions.

During therapy I began to realize how boring I was, and it used to embarrass me. How could the therapist *stand* to listen to the drivel? Because it's mostly drivel that you speak—it's not interesting dialogue written by Graham Greene. And he had to sit and listen to exactly the same sort of thing eight times a day for an hour each session, sometimes more, every day of his life. One time in the middle of our session he got an emergency phone call. One of his patients was desperate. But I could tell from what I could hear from my side that it was boring my therapist, even though here was a man on the phone who was about to commit suicide. The doctor was saying, "Well, I'll be here in my office, and I'll wait until eight-thirty if you want to see me." He kept his voice calm and he tried to quiet the man.

I can envision another situation in which the therapist is sitting there and a woman is telling him of her lifelong struggle with her sister. "My sister's always been jealous of me; she's hated me all her life"—and she goes through this in detail for four hundred sessions. Four hundred sessions talking about her sister! Imagine having to put up with that!

I used to tell the shrink jokes all the time just to make him laugh. I could make him laugh until he cried. I've always used that as a form of acceptance. If I can make people laugh, I feel I've won their approval; they're glad to be with me. Many performers have the same background: they were the class clown in school and so forth.

I remember exactly what the most surprising insight about myself was. I asked the therapist why I had this terrible urge all the time to be "on," to be the center of attention. If I was at a party I'd talk: I always talk too much. When the shrink asked my why, I said, "Well, if I just sit in a corner and don't say anything I'm a schmuck." And he said, "Look: you don't have to be the big *macher* and you don't have to be a schmuck.

There's something in between." That was a revelation for me!

About ten years after I finished therapy, my shrink called me up one day. He said he was revising all his own theories about treatment, questioning all his tenets, beliefs and doctrines and wondering whether there was any genuine, pragmatic value in treatment. So he was looking up all his old patients to see if they could honestly say they were better. I told him I believed I truly was, and that seemed to give him a great deal of reassurance and pleasure.

But I didn't realize he was going downhill himself very fast at that time. He carried a tremendous workload. I suppose he was working eighteen hours a day. And he started taking Dexedrine to keep going. They did not know then that Dex was that dangerous; I remember taking it, too. It did so much brain damage, I was told by a former colleague of his, that he literally could not function, and that was the end of him. He committed suicide.

I had been very, very happy with the man, and I had a very fine relationship with him. Finally, though, we had reached a point where I felt I was standing on my own two feet, so to speak, and I didn't think I could get much more out of the therapy. The shrink seemed terribly pleased.

Success changes you. One of my problems in the past was intense anxiety about ever making it in my profession. I think that treatment helped me to make it, gave me more confidence in myself; but if I hadn't made it—and this is such a chancy business—*no* amount of treatment would have saved me; I'd be suicidal again. I don't think I could have taken it.

My entire *amour-propre,* my entire pride in myself, whatever self-respect, self-esteem or macho I have, is based entirely on my ability as an actor. Acceptance by others as a fine actor. You could tell me I'm a rotten citizen, a rotten lover, a rotten traitor, or the lowest thing in the world: it wouldn't bother me. I would just think, "What the hell do you know?" But tell me I'm a bad actor and you've killed me. I can't take it. It's the only thing I have any pride in. I don't think of myself as anything but an actor: that's all I am.

Rex Reed

Rex Reed is a nationally syndicated critic and the author of such books as *Do You Sleep in the Nude?*, *People Are Crazy Here,* and *Valentines & Vitriol.* He is also the film critic for *Vogue* magazine.

About eight years ago I was doing an interview with Tony Perkins, who was in analysis with a woman named Mildred Newman. He said, "Well, you're in worse shape than I am"—because I was talking a little bit about myself—and he asked, "Would you go to see somebody if I arranged it? Maybe she won't even have time to take you; maybe you won't even go a second time, but would you just go?"

Well, I was really ready for therapy at that time, and I said yes. And I went to Mildred, and I've been going to her ever since. It's been of tremendous help. It's really taught me to be on my own team. I've gotten more from it than I ever thought I'd get.

What she did was just help me to say "Fuck you" to the world. I mean, I don't care what anybody thinks now. That's one thing I really *had* to learn. You—not somebody else—have got to be number one in your life.

I used to turn on talk shows and see people talking about me who didn't even know me. And I would take their side when they'd be saying, "He's a monster." I'd say, "Oh, they're right, they're right. I have no business being a critic." I was becoming very neurotic and very gun-shy. It disturbed me that anybody would have an opinion about me that they would be airing publicly without knowing me. Also, I resented the fact that they didn't understand that this was a job I was doing and that it wasn't personal. I would just go into such a decline. I would have stomach trouble, throw up and everything else.

Now I've learned to live with criticism. How people react to my work is their problem. I couldn't care less. I just laugh. I've learned to separate the public image people have of me from the person I really am—and you have to do that. So many people who become well known overnight can't differentiate between what the public thinks of them and what they think of themselves. Being a critic is just a job; it has nothing to do with getting along in society. I went into therapy because I was really experiencing a lot of pain, adjusting to the sudden public image that people were giving me.

I was just somebody who really made it in journalism very

quickly, and suddenly I was a public figure and didn't want to be. This was because I didn't think I had changed at all, and I didn't want people to think I had. Other people start doing big trips and heavy numbers on you about how you've changed. And it's really just them—they're the ones who are doing the changing.

There are different kinds of analysis. There's the kind that tries to change you and make you a better person. And then there's the kind of analysis that helps you to live with your own neuroses and use them as part of your life. This is the kind of analysis I've had.

It was hard opening up in the beginning. I didn't really think my problems were of interest to anyone else but me. I thought they were all very minor. I thought you had to be Blanche Dubois to go into analysis, or somebody who's really totally berserk. I just knew that I wasn't happy and I wasn't getting enough out of life. I wasn't really enjoying my success, and I wanted to find out if it was my fault or somebody else's.

I never felt any hostility toward Mildred at all. I was just so grateful to find someone I could open up to and talk to the way other people were opening up and talking to me about *their* problems. Because I had no one to talk to about my own insecurities. And that's what I got most out of my therapy with Mildred. She was a total friend.

That's the magic she has, of making you feel completely wanted, needed, valuable and vital. Instantly. You establish such a friendship with her that you would tell her anything.

She knows what kind of mood I'm in the minute I walk in. She can tell by the way I look.

She treats each person individually. I think that's very good, because it makes you feel that you're not part of a flock of people she's applying some general theory to. You're an individual, and she has to work with you on whatever level she thinks is important to you. She establishes an immediate rapport and an immediate trust, which is very hard to do. I know people who have been in analysis for years and years and they hate their analyst and they drop out and go to another one. This goes on for fifteen or twenty years, and they've had a string of analysts, and they don't have anything good to say about any of them. This is not the way it is with Mildred.

All a good analyst can do is provide you with the raw materials and give you the weapons to go out and live in society. But they can't live your life for you. The real pitfall is coming to depend on your analyst as a crutch. Which is what I find so many people in show business do. I mean, I know a lot of actors who call their analysts from backstage in the middle of a rehearsal, saying, "So-and-so just yelled at me. What do I do?" And they're in tears. That is really not learning to be an adult at all. It's just using the analyst as a substitute for a mother or father. And I'm sure a lot of people do that with Mildred, too, but I never did. She was always just a great friend, and still is.

It was hard for me to understand right off the bat why certain insecurities I had stemmed from certain childhood roots that I thought I had forgotten and written out of my life. But they were still responsible for the adult problems I was having. Until I could work out those problems I couldn't really work out the adult problems. And it was hard to go back and get in touch with childhood feelings.

I never really had any peers. I never had any people my own age that I could relate to, so it was very difficult for me to consider myself valuable to any group of people my age. I was not programmed for acceptance, because I never had any when I was growing up. I was always with adults. So here I am an adult and I don't believe other adults like me or believe what I say or care about what I say. I felt like a child in an adult world. And that was one of my problems. And of course it had to do with growing up the way I did, moving constantly.

The most difficult thing has been learning to rely on myself. I was spending my whole life waiting to find somebody who would have all the answers and would just sort of be an adult and allow me to be a child. But now I realize that that's not possible or realistic, and I wouldn't be happy if I did have that. So in analysis I've been learning how to be my own boss and the person I have to answer to, as well as my own best friend.

How to Be Your Own Best Friend is the title of the book Mildred Newman wrote. It doesn't matter what anybody thinks about that title; it is the most truthful book I've ever read, and it puts forth the philosophy I care about most. It's the philosophy I have learned, and it has really changed my life and my whole way of thinking about myself.

The main thing to remember is that the worst thing you think about yourself is not so terrible. All you need is somebody else to say, "So what? That's the worst? Wait'll I tell you about myself."

Previously I just sort of assumed the blame for things. If I was stopped by a traffic cop, in my own mind I was automatically guilty of everything. Every time I walked out of a department store, I thought, "I wonder if they think I'm stealing something. I wonder if that cop at the door thinks I've got something in this shopping bag." I just automatically assumed that other people would think I was guilty, because I really didn't have much self-respect.

I was always thinking, "Such and such a writer would have written this better than I did," or "So-and-so would have phrased this differently, but I just can't think of any other way to write it, so I must not be a good writer." That was because I didn't really have a very strong foundation in journalism. I never thought I was as good as other people. That's why I really stopped reading other writers for a long time. And even now I don't read too much journalism. I rarely read a profile of anyone. It's just not good to have too much admiration for other people. It makes it difficult for you to do your own work.

I got to the point where I was putting off everything because I just didn't think it would be as good as I wanted it to be. I'm still my own worst critic. I'm pretty tough on myself as far as my work goes, but I still stand by it.

I guess the most difficult thing for my friends is that I never have any free time, and they can never get my undivided attention, because my mind is always somewhere else. It's always on some deadline or something that I have to achieve but that I don't really *want* to achieve. I'm doing a lot of assignments for the money. That's another thing. It's not a totally fulfilling job I'm doing, because I'm trying also to make some money.

My biggest problem is that I do not have time for anything frivolous. I don't have time to chat with friends on the phone or to meet them for drinks in restaurants or to have dinners that go on until eleven o'clock at night. I have no time for any of that. I've always got a deadline facing me, or I have to be present somewhere where there is some kind of story to be gotten out of my presence there. I mean, I always have either to be at a play I don't want to see—because I have to write about it—or to go to a screening of a movie I know I'm going to hate—because I have to write about it.

I mean, don't forget: I'm on the radio four times a day on CBS, I have these two columns a week that have to be written, and I'm the movie critic for *Vogue* magazine. I have deadlines facing me constantly. And I don't have time to just take the afternoon off and go to the beach. I will be in school forever, as long as I'm a writer. There will always be school, and there will always be a test—and this is just something I hate. But I wasn't born rich, so I have to do what I can do to make some money. If I weren't doing it at all I would be unhappy, so I can't really complain too much. But if it weren't for the money, I would do it much less. I would skip an awful lot, but I wouldn't be making the money I'm making now.

With Mildred the main topic of conversation is whatever you need to talk about. I spend more time talking about my problems with my profession than anything else.

Sometimes I don't go. Usually it's because I don't have anything to talk about. Nothing is progressing, and I feel I'm sort of in the same condition I was in the week before. Most of the time it's because I've done nothing but work all week and haven't seen one person, haven't had one conflict, don't have anything to ask her to help me solve—so I just feel that going to see her would be a waste of time. But most of the time I go anyway, or we'll have a session on the phone.

My therapy has given me a much more analytical approach personally to my life and to the lives of others and to my work. I just think it's made me a wiser and much more well-rounded person. I'll never discount that. I think that's a very valuable thing to learn how to be.

Now if I'm depressed I just try to think positively about everything. I try to analyze it more carefully. "Why am I feeling low? Where is this coming from?" And I try to deal with it then instead of putting it off. I used to have this philosophy that "Tomorrow everything will be better. I'll wake up tomorrow and my whole life will be changed." I don't do that now. I try to deal with the problem at the time it's happening to me.

I think I've become more compassionate about other people. In interviewing people now I don't form instant opinions of them as easily as I used to. I'm much more compassionate about people who have a lot of draining problems and a lot of insecurities. I used to really have no tolerance at all for insecurity. I didn't understand why anybody who was famous was insecure—but now I do understand.

Famous people are right out there in the public eye all the time. Everybody's watching you pick your nose. Everybody's after you for everything. Nobody calls Mrs. Smith and asks her to send her blouse or her book or her jewelry to a cause for arthritic children. Nobody does that to ordinary people. But my phone never stops ringing. And you just have to learn how to deal with these people instead of running away from them.

You know why all these magazines like *People* are so popular and why all of the gossip columns are proliferating now to such a rapid degree? It's because people love their own anonymity but they love to read about people who are famous. It's all the things they never will be—but how lucky they are. They wouldn't want to be these other people, really. They just want to read about their miseries. It's easier if you have no public identity.

There are little personal habits of mine that I'd like to change. I mean, no one will believe I'm basically a very lazy person, but I am. I would like to be much more disciplined than I am. I put everything off. Even if I have a five-month deadline on a story, I will be up all night the night before it's due, writing it. When I was in college I'd put everything off until the night before a test, and then I would start on page one of the textbook. It's always been like that, and I just hate it. But I don't seem to be very organized.

I've always been a very opinionated person, and I'm always willing to talk about my opinions. But when it comes to talking about myself, I find it difficult. That's why I don't do interviews much anymore. And the question of analysis has always been something very personal that I've needed to work out because I was just not a very happy person. And I'm still working all the time and have no private life to speak of, but at least I think I'm capable of having a private life now, which I didn't before.

The main thing I've learned out of all this is that at this point in my life I don't want to be anybody else. When I was little I wanted to be Fred Astaire, but I couldn't dance. I was always very clumsy. I'm still a very bad dancer. When I started acting I wanted to be James Dean, but I wasn't really right for any of the parts he would have played—or that Monty Clift would have played. I became a writer and I wanted to be J. D. Salinger, so I started writing like him. Then I wanted to be Truman Capote, so I started writing like *him*. I'm a very good imitator of styles: I can drift in and out of one style and then another. It's taken me all this time to realize that I can just write whatever I want to write my way and that will be me. I don't have to *be* anybody else. Now people are always saying that I have a lot of imitators, and that, I suppose, is a form of flattery. I don't really care what they're doing, though; I just care about getting my own work done and getting on with it and having some kind of time left over for myself.

Elizabeth Ashley

Elizabeth Ashley spoke with me in her suite at the Beverly Hills Hotel. Dressed in a colorful print blouse, white pants and sandals, she projected a strikingly attractive image that was enhanced by an alluring southern accent and the sharp intelligence which underlay her words.

Besides the mandatory script—which is almost always somewhere in evidence around people who make their living in the world of make-believe—her coffee table abounded with books, including Lillian Hellman's *Scoundrel Time* and Tennessee Williams's *Memoirs.* Elizabeth Ashley is well read, and one senses an appealing curiosity on her part about the world around her.

Ashley scored her first success at twenty-two, winning a Tony Award as Art Carney's daughter in *Take Her, She's Mine.* Soon after, she had a starring role in *Barefoot in the Park.* In 1975 she triumphed again on Broadway in a smash-hit revival of *Cat on a Hot Tin Roof.* Her films have included *Ship of Fools* and *The Carpetbaggers.* She was previously married to actors James Farentino and George Peppard.

Toward the end of our chat, her husband, Tom McCarthy, returned to the suite, but his presence seemed to have little effect on her rapid-fire and blush-proof stream of comment.

She told me that she enjoys her life immensely, apparently having more or less sorted out its various elements. The role that therapy played in helping her achieve her present sense of well being is one which she admits unhesitatingly.

When I was very young, and had never been anywhere north of Georgia, I found myself in New York City: lost, frightened, and in pain. It reached a point where, before I could cross a street, I would stand and shake. I couldn't put sentences together. I was in such pain emotionally that the terror from the pain became unbearable.

A friend of mine, a boy whom I was going out with, had a sister who was in therapy with a psychologist. I began to see that psychologist on a regular basis, and it helped me. I began to feel better, which is the biggest help that anyone or anything can ever give you.

I had been kind of lost and had never found a place for myself. I had never felt comfortable on the planet from the time I arrived on it. Unless you fit into a niche in your culture, then you are outside of it. And if you live outside of your culture, particularly as a child, there's enormous pressure put on you to find your nook or cranny. If you don't, there's something "wrong" with you.

The first thing animals do if they are uncomfortable or under stress or in pain of any kind is to physically move. I made a number of physical moves, but the demons were still there. So I then had to move in other kinds of ways, one of which was going to a psychologist.

About three years after I started seeing the psychologist, I had a nervous breakdown. They put me in Payne-Whitney and I started seeing an analyst. This was when I was about twenty-two, after I had become a big success. I had enormous general and abstract, all-pervading guilt all the time because I'd never been able to accomplish or achieve anything. I'd always been a failure at everything all my life.

You're conditioned to believe that you're going to get punished. Somehow you think you'll make brownie points with God if you flail yourself rather than waiting for somebody else to do it.

I would generally accomplish this through relationships. I would get into relationships that were going to hurt me one way or another. I would want more from the relationship than was possible. Or I would get into love affairs with people who would punish me for the reasons that my life had always punished me: that I couldn't fit in, that I couldn't do all the things it was thought one was supposed to do.

The people I'd get involved with would not value at all what I did do but value enormously that which I could not do. And be very possessive and demanding and authoritarian.

So I always wound up—from the time when I was very young—in relationships that would be pretty destructive for anybody but deeply destructive for me. It wasn't enough that I had myself punishing myself; I would always find somebody else to do it, too.

I would be with people who might want me or even love me but who could not like me or approve of me. I was constantly in relationships with men like this, which reinforced my feeling that I was bad.

I've never been addicted to substances—other than cigarettes—but I was emotionally addictive. And there are emotional drugs that are just as addictive as material ones, and I was forever feeding my needs. But I did it less and less. You change organically, which is the miracle of analysis when it's good (or at its best) and works. Organically your emotional reflexes change in time, and that's why analysis is a long, arduous, day-in, day-out structured process.

Another way in which analysis changed my life with men radically was finding out that what was always held up as what a man is is a really barbaric thing. I mean, as hard as it is for a woman in our culture, I think it's harder for a man.

I think the male image and the male role are as barbaric and dehumanizing and horrific as anything. Most men have been conditioned, unfortunately, to think that their earning power and their testicles are somehow related. They think success is what they're placed on this earth for, and is how they're measured.

I found out that the strongest men are the ones who are not frightened of their frailties, who accept them totally. And a man who accepts his frailties also accepts his strengths; consequently, he can accept my strengths and my frailties.

I understand that a lot of men are going to have a violent, visceral negative reaction to a woman like me—or who they think I am—and I don't take it personally. I'm too old to get into street fights, so I'm really fast and slippery, and I just glide on by.

I no longer attempt even conversation with men who are committed to the system and to working within it in any sense. I can't live my life within it; I live on the outside edges. I live with carnival people and the outlaws—and by my own choice. It's the only place I've ever wanted to be—and I've found it's a be-able place.

I live my life now the way I want to—rather guilt-free—and have a better time and more enviable life than anybody I know. I mean, I wouldn't trade my life in on anybody else's that I've ever even heard about. I think the only responsibility I have is to put a great deal back into the world in whatever small ways I can, because I get a great deal out of it. I don't fight so much anymore in my work or personal life, because I don't need to. I suppose I'm not as angry, not as defensive.

I went to a psychologist and three analysts before I found the analyst who was right for me. Not many people have the proclivity for being paternal-maternal wise men, and that's the station that therapists or analysts really occupy in our culture.

I think going through therapy is a very difficult thing to do, and the only reason to do it is if you're in so much pain or you're having so much trouble in your life that you can't get out of it any other way.

You pay that fifty or sixty dollars an hour whether you show or not. It's not an extracurricular activity. It must organically become central to your life if, in fact, it is going to affect your life in any lasting way. Otherwise, go talk to a friend, or somebody who will give you band-aids. Go to one of those seminars for a weekend: that's an extracurricular activity.

In trying to find the right analyst, I don't think we should take anything on face value. One should go in skeptically, which is hard to do when you're in pain. But because it's your life you're talking about, you should be as careful with this as anything you ever do in your life.

I was in analysis with a man whose values and standards were very different from mine—or what mine came to be, in growing and maturing. So, consequently, there could never be any agreement between us, essentially because I disapproved deeply of his values, his life-style and so forth—and he, I'm sure, disapproved of mine. So I had to find an analyst with whom I could be comfortable.

It wasn't necessary to find an analyst *like* me, but I wanted to feel that my values and standards, my dreams, the things I cherished and loved, the things I held in contempt and my code of morality—that these things were not in direct conflict or being held in contempt by someone whose own sense of values I did not particularly value.

After three years with this last analyst, I had gotten to a point past which I couldn't seem to get with him. I just sort of finished with him and went on living my life. About a year or so later, I wanted some help emotionally. I was in a lot of crises in my life—there were a lot of impasses—and I needed to find out how to support myself emotionally. So I saw a number of analysts and finally met a woman about whom I had a different sort of feeling. It was all visceral, but of course I'm supposed to know more about this type of thing than other people because it's how I earn my living.

I stayed with this lady for about four years, and that's the last time I've gone through analysis. I haven't been in treatment since 1970.

My advice to anyone who is ever going to go for any kind of therapy or treatment is to get the best person you can find. I mean, this is not an area in which you go cut-rate ever. It's not a place to go for what is faddish or trendy: this tendency is something that is so full of dangers that it terrifies me.

Find someone you feel comfortable with. It doesn't have to do with what you think: it has to do with what you feel. You're there because of what you feel.

There is a danger always that the analyst or therapist has somehow got an abstract concept of what an adjusted human being is. He may say, "We have to fit Jane Doe into this space, for her to be a healthy human being," which is an approach I totally disagree with.

Psychoanalysis is the most totally unique relationship in the world, because eventually, in a constructive analysis, you will relate to the analyst as you relate to every situation, every circumstance, every human being and every primal feeling you've ever had.

You'll go through the whole spectrum, your whole repertoire: everything you've ever known, everything you've ever felt, every reaction you've ever had, every way you've ever felt about anybody in your life, you will eventually feel about the analyst. That's one of the reasons for the couch and not talking directly eye-to-eye: it's important to cease to need to measure reactions. That's also why stream of consciousness, which is visceral, rather than conversation, which is intellectual.

I suppose I'm an emotional exhibitionist anyway, because of what I do for a living. I've never felt that the outpouring or explosion of emotion is harmful: you can hurt people's feelings or hurt situations, but generally the damage that is done is probably supposed to be done. Because to repress rage, anger, fear or love makes them like boils. You've got a choice in this life: either you've got an open, running sore that's a boil you can see, or you've got an ulcer that you can't.

The first stuff that comes out is easy. It gets harder and harder the deeper you go. You go for the longest period of time and you can't think of anything to say. You go through all your repertoire: you try to elicit a response or pick a fight or go for shock value or any kind of prod—but with a good analyst, you won't get anything.

A surprising thing is finding out that information is not cure. I think that I, like many other people, grew up with the assumption that if you could just find out enough stuff, then you could figure everything out.

But one's emotional life has very little to do with one's mental or intellectual life. And being able to uncover and look at many of the things that were my particular demons did not alter the habits and patterns of a lifetime, the hungers that we are born with and develop on our journey in life.

Neurosis should not be confused with madness. One's madnesses one should cling to, because they generally are at the same place as one's passions and dreams and gods—and nothing on earth is strong enough to deeply interfere with those things. It's only a matter of making peace, so that you can spend enough time vertical each day out doing whatever you have to do so they don't come and get you. Because we live in a society where they'll kill you if you don't play by the rules. The maverick, the loner, the outlaw is becoming less and less tolerated here in the land of the free and the home of the brave.

I think it's very important to question the culture you live in. I got to that place that's an old cliché: If the world is sane, then I am crazy. If, on the other hand, I am sane, then the world has surely gone mad. And that's what I feel. I feel benevolent and compassionate toward a world that has gone mad. And I consider myself privileged and blessed, because I feel that I'm not one more lemming. Simple.

I think the science of psychotherapy, even though it is a pioneer one, has served culture in the sense that it stripped taboos off certain kinds of dialogue. It became the trendy thing to do for a while. Unfortunately, now it's filtered down to where it's in franchises, as I understand it. I don't know anything about most of this type of thing, but I do know that you can't franchise, you can't have Kentucky Colonel stands of emotional solace to help emotional pain. But, on the other hand, if you think something helps you, it helps you. So it will be interesting to see where it all goes.

Therapy is a stage, and it lasts as long as it needs to. There are some people who have been so wounded just by being alive that they're like a diabetic: they're going to have to get that insulin shot for the rest of their lives just to stay even. Some people can go for six months to deal with something. Some people go into therapy only to find out for sure that they don't need it. It's always an individual thing.

For me the hardest part of therapy was just showing up, because I resented the routine. It's a structure. When I go to work, I have to fix my hair, put on makeup, get dressed up, show up on time, sweat, work and do as I'm told. So I am very, very careful never, ever to do any of those things any other place in my life—that's the only way I can keep my life balanced. If I adhered to any kind of social behavior, then I would be doing double time. What you see is what you get. I pretend for a living; I don't pretend for free. I don't owe the world any more pretense. I'm like the United Fund: I over-give that way every time I go to work.

I would love to be wiser than I am. I have a terrible mouth. My sense of humor usually manifests itself in absolutely outrageous smart-mouthing, and I wish I could outgrow that a little bit.

In work situations I tend to overdramatize and overstate my case. I've also got to learn to hang out and be a bum more: I mean, there's no reward in heaven (necessarily) for the laborer. I've got to learn to have a better time all the time. I used to be absolutely insufferable because I had no sense of humor at all about my work.

My sex life improved beyond my wildest dreams as a result of analysis, as it always does when you love yourself. The more you love yourself, the better every aspect of your life will be.

If I couldn't solve a problem for myself now, I would immediately go back for a five-thousand-mile checkup—with no hesitation. I don't feel that it's falling from grace to have the sweats and the shakes and the screams at four A. M.—I figure it's part of living. And if the time comes when I get them very consistently at four A. M. and I can't figure out why and get myself off that hook, I'll go for help. I'll get help anywhere I can, any way I can, for any pain I've got in this life. I don't believe in the Calvinist ethic that suffering is good; I just don't.

Bob Newhart

It was unusually warm and magnificent in Hollywood this late November day, and Bob Newhart wished aloud that he were on the golf course rather than at CBS's Studio Center, where he would be working until early into the night. But the sixteenth episode of *The Bob Newhart Show,* then in its fourth season, would be shot in twenty-four hours, and Newhart and his TV cohorts were spending the day running through this next-to-last rehearsal before performing in front of a live audience Friday night.

Outside the tastefully furnished dressing room where we talked was a doormat which read "Bob Newhart—Don Rickles' Best Friend." Inside were several mementos of Newhart's friendship with that other comedian whose style so differs from the subtle, deadpan approach that characterizes his own.

Newhart's off-screen persona is strikingly similar to the one he projects publicly; he is polite, soft-spoken and unassuming. At lunch in the studio commissary, Newhart called greetings to technicians and crew members, addressing all by first names and making a personal inquiry of each.

Dressed as he was in a short-sleeved white knit sport shirt, white pants and sneakers, it was not difficult to imagine Newhart in the role of a midwestern accountant, which indeed he was before he decided that comedy was his forte. But his distinctive delivery—which is in evidence even when he speaks in dead earnest—reminded me immediately that this ex-CPA is now another man, one who brings laughter into millions of American homes every Saturday night.

The reason our show (which concerns a psychologist) is successful today—and it couldn't have been five years ago—is that people today realize that sometimes there are problems they face which they can't solve themselves because there are so many intertwined things that get in the way. And talking to Mrs. Murphy over the back fence isn't always the best solution, because she may have just had a fight with her husband, and it may not be the best time to hit her.

I think some people use psychiatry as a fad, or as a status symbol. But there is a time when you need the help of somebody who's trained, a shrink. When you say certain things, he hears them differently than a good friend, who doesn't know how to ask the right question or listen for the right answer.

I guess there are certain signs that tell you when you need to get professional help, but I don't know what they are. I would think that just being unable to cope with a situation might justify seeking some help.

My fear of flying was the primary reason I went. It got to be a hassle. I wound up taking trains all the time, and most of the people on trains these days are eighty years old. They talk about Hoover and what a great President he was, which doesn't leave me much to contribute to the conversation. So I wind up going into the club car and getting bombed by three o'clock.

Even when I understood the cause of my fear of flying—it came from a childhood experience when I was kind of trapped in this small area for a few minutes—it didn't dissipate. But my fear now is the alternative, the giving in to the fear, which would mean not going anywhere. So you get on an airplane and you're not comfortable: there are a lot of situations you're not comfortable in, but the alternative is worse. Now I find I'm flying more, even taking private planes.

The fear of flying is not unusual among celebrities, because they tend to be in control of situations the rest of the time. A comedian, especially, is totally in control of his material. If it isn't working, you get out of it and into something that *is* working. Or if something is working, you continue on with it and stretch it as far as you can. So, on airplanes, aside from the claustrophobia, you experience a loss of control. On a private plane you don't quite have the same thing: you can always go up and check the speed and the height.

The other reason I went into therapy is that things were getting in the way of everything being as pleasant as it should be. I had a tendency to put myself in the middle of situations and negate courses of action, so there would be no way out for me. I was constantly putting myself in a box without realizing it. I suppose this involved some sort of guilt, which made me feel I shouldn't enjoy things that I had been taught, at least, were the things I would want to be happy. I'm talking about material things. It's a way of saying, "Sure, you think I have everything, but look at this." It's just a guilt that you carry around with you for one reason or another. It's a form of mental masochism, I suppose.

What I found out that surprised me was that I allowed myself to be maneuvered into situations that I really didn't want to be in. I had a terrible fear of offending people—and it's pretty hard to go through life without offending people.

One day I told the shrink that my wife and I were going out to dinner that night even though I really didn't want to be with the people we were meeting. So he asked me, "Well, why are you going out with them?" Now, there are two different ways you can interpret this type of question. One is that he's giving approval, saying, "No, you don't have to go out with them." The other possibility is that he is asking you the question, "Why do you feel you have to go out with these people? What is it in your character that makes you afraid of offending them?"

It's a funny thing, an odd thing that happens in analysis: you mistake the shrink's questioning for approval, which of course doesn't necessarily make it right. I mean, the approval has to come from inside, not outside.

At any rate, now I handle these social things differently. Now I say, "I don't want to go there." We have a situation that we're going through now with some people who invited us out. We really have little enough time to ourselves and our children as it is, because of various things we *have* to do, things that are almost mandatory. So I don't want to acquire any new friends that I'm going to have to spend time with, and I don't feel particularly guilty about this.

These people we're having the problem with are really marginal acquaintances; since they put us in this situation with them, we shouldn't be worried about offending them. I guess this represents a change in my thinking. I'm not as concerned about offending people. I'm not just saying "the hell with everybody," but there are certain situations I want to avoid, and I'm just saying "No," whereas previously I wouldn't have.

I find on the set of my show that I say certain things I didn't used to say. "I don't like this script. It may hurt your feelings, but I don't like it." If I *didn't* say this, they would presume I liked the script and there might be another like it.

It's easier not to say anything, but you find you're not enjoying yourself as much as you should. Now I find I'm happier.

I was raised in the kind of family where we didn't argue. I remember one time I was having a session with the therapist and I said if I did a certain thing, my wife Ginny and I would get into a fight. And he said, "Well, what's wrong with a fight?" Like "Why are you afraid of getting into a fight?" Some very productive things come out of fights; they're not pleasant to go through, but they can be beneficial.

There's more openness now between me and my wife. I think we have a much better relationship now than we did. I think the first five or six years of marriage are very tough, because people are finding out about each other. You find out you're not going to change anybody. You learn to live with each other's limitations.

I had a problem with the open display of affection. Ginny tends to be very affectionate and I tend to be less so. I tend to by very controlled, which I don't particularly like in myself: I wish I were more the other way. And I think that's changed. We also became friends with Don Rickles and his wife. Don is very outgoing and very affectionate. He hugs and says "Gee, it's great to see you; we really missed you," et cetera. I think that affected me somewhat. It makes it much more pleasant for me.

I think the reason I'm not as affectionate as I should be is because I'm actually more affected by situations than many others. If I allowed myself to be openly affected by them, then I'd spend most of my time *being* affected by them.

It's almost like living in New York. They say in *Future Shock* that people in New York aren't cold; they're just saying, "You have to understand. I wish I could help you, but if I stop to help you I will never get to work, because there are so many things going on around me that are upsetting me that if I allow them to intrude on me, I won't accomplish anything."

I made the movie *Catch-22*, and one of the guys on the picture, an actor, said that all he lived for was to go to his analyst. He wanted to go all day, not take jobs or anything, but lie on the shrink's couch and let it all flow. I couldn't imagine looking forward to that kind of thing.

One guy, a producer in New York, told me that he was married to this woman who was terribly neurotic, and he talked her into going to a psychiatrist. He found out afterwards that it was only her neuroses that attracted him at all, and when she got rid of those, she was totally unattractive to him.

I read recently that the American Psychological Association said that if there's a psychiatrist who believes that sex is therapeutic, he should be required to say beforehand, up front, that he has this tendency to jump on his patients. And I think he shouldn't limit it to just attractive ones; if he feels it's helpful, then he should spread it around. Personally I think it's somewhat suspect.

My therapist was recommended by my wife's therapist. I stayed with the guy the whole time because I wasn't aware of any problems. I was perfectly content with him. He was a very nice man. There are charlatans in the field—maybe more in this field than any other. But I didn't feel that the one I was going to was a charlatan.

I asked him once, "How do you pick a psychiatrist?" In the Yellow Pages you have "Psychiatrists," but what do you do—

pick out a name you like the sound of? If a restaurant serves good food, it's always crowded; if a body shop does good work, it's always busy. But with shrinks there's no waiting line. How can you say somebody's cured or who has the best percentage of curing people? It's only by hearsay. There are a lot of kooks in the profession who are doing more harm than good: they're getting people who are moderately screwed up and making them tremendously screwed up. I've run into people who went to psychiatrists and are really fucked up, really in bad shape—and unaware of it.

The toughest part of therapy for me was reliving some of the painful moments that everybody has, rejection and things like that. They weren't pleasant to begin with, and to have to go through them again was really unpleasant. I'm talking about things everybody goes through, in high school and college, that kind of thing. In a way, though, I felt better after recounting some of these experiences, because now there was another person who knew.

I think the break-in at the office of Daniel Ellsberg's psychiatrist affected me, and I think it affected a lot of people. I mean, I wondered, "Is what I'm saying private, and will it remain private? And if it won't remain private, then let me couch it in the most attractive terms." Certainly in my position now there's no reason for anyone to go into my shrink's offices, but such offices have been bugged.

The caution concerning what you say also has something to do with the kind of life you lead. When you're being interviewed by a newspaper reporter, you tend to visualize what you're saying in print. You wonder what it's going to sound like, so you're constantly editing—and I found myself editing in the sessions.

I told my shrink one day, "There are some things I'm not going to tell you, but I will never tell anybody. I want that, my own private thing." So I guess there was a fear he might invade those areas. I think my shrink was hurt a little bit; I guess he thought he had failed as a psychiatrist in not getting that ultimate trust. It wasn't even a fear on my part of shock, that I would shock him with what I was going to say. It's just that it was something that was mine and private and not for anybody else.

I also told the shrink that I was Catholic, wished to remain Catholic and didn't want him, if he didn't happen to be religious, to attempt to impose his personal preferences on me.

There were many times when I didn't want to go. Some of it was because we were just going over the same area that we had gone over before. Sometimes it was really not having anything to tell him that day, or not thinking I had anything to tell him. Of course, psychiatrists say those are the most productive sessions, when you don't want to go, because you're moving to a plateau you don't want to reach.

One instance when you get strong feelings about the shrink is when you're not seeing any progress, when you're saying, "OK, I understand this, so why can't I stop doing it?" Another thing that's frustrating is his lack of emotion, which is what he's been trained all these years not to show.

The people you're talking to for this book are, almost to a man or a woman, insecure people who tend to get into acting or performing because there's something in us we don't like. There's some kind of guilt; we don't like ourselves as people, so it's more fun to be somebody else. It's especially true with impressionists; they think people find them more acceptable as Burt Lancaster or Spencer Tracy.

I think the maturity happens finally when you realize why you perform. I found I do it now because I enjoy making people laugh. I mean, I think there are a lot of other reasons I used to do it; to be more socially acceptable was one reason. I think now I do it because I genuinely enjoy making people laugh: it's a satisfaction.

The only fear I had was that somehow analysis would interfere with the creative process, which I don't completely understand. I don't know why I write a particular line or why it sounds funny or why I time it this way or that way. I was concerned that in becoming healthier, possibly I would lose my sense of humor. And I really can't go back to accounting at this point. My subscription to *Accounting Monthly* lapsed several years ago, and I'm really not up to date on many of the changes. Plus there's a certain life-style I've grown accustomed to.

I think every comedian lives with the fear that one day he's going to go to a nightclub and it's going to be empty. And it's going to happen overnight: they're just going to say, "We don't care to see you anymore." I'm not sure this isn't true with any performer. It's not a real worry, but I think you're always amazed that *anybody* showed up, and upset that more people didn't. It's a dichotomy that you live with.

I think the whole experience of therapy was painful at first but, looking back now at where I was, pleasurable, because I like where I am now and I didn't like where I was before. The shrink helped me get to the point where I am today. It's made my life better: I've gotten to know myself better, and I like myself a little more.

Dom DeLuise

"Keep calling me, and be aggressive about it," Dom DeLuise had advised when I first phoned about setting up a meeting. His schedule—like so many others'—was jammed, and my best bet to corner him was to follow his advice. So I kept calling. And when a break in the shooting of the movie *Sextette*, in which he appears with Mae West, gave him an unanticipated day at home, he was on the line telling me to hurry on down to his place in Pacific Palisades.

His dog began barking at the sound of the doorbell, and I heard a familiar voice shout "Kill!" But DeLuise was smiling benevolently when he answered my ring and led me into his ranch-style house.

Barefoot and wearing a baby blue kimono-style terry cloth robe, the comedian fidgeted with the plastic covering of a place mat as we sat at the round wooden table that fills his breakfast room.

Alternately serious and playful, he would sometimes finish a response with an unexpected punchline or do a fast bit of *shtick*, once raising his voice in an unintelligible Italian dialect to convey a sense of his father's anger. But behind humor there is often pain. In Dom DeLuise's case, the pain led him into therapy—an experience, he has concluded, that saved his life.

People go into therapy, I think, when they're unhappy with themselves or they're not functioning correctly. If you're having a lot of trouble with your marriage or a lot of trouble relating to people or just a lot of trouble being with yourself—which is ultimately the thing you have to deal with—then you seek some help.

Our mind is a funny thing. If a child is bitten by a dog, every time he sees a dog he gets frightened. As intellectual, rational human beings we know that not all dogs are killers, but how can you explain it to our minds? Sometimes we have to outthink our minds because our minds can fuck us up. The mind records incorrectly sometimes.

I got involved in therapy because I wasn't functioning very well and I was feeling like I wasn't a good person. My behavior was always sweet—like a pussycat's—but I started to think I was a much more base person than I was giving the picture of. I thought that I behaved as if I liked children on the outside, but inside, probably, I didn't like them. "What's the reason I'm being nice to my mother? Am I being nice to her because I want everybody to think I'm a nice guy? *Am* I really a nice guy?" So I went to a doctor and I found out, after a while, that I was a nice guy, *truly* a nice guy.

A child learns very, very quickly to hold back his feelings, his anger. Your mother will slap you; your father will yell at you and scream at you if you let out your anger. Sometimes even too much joy can get you in trouble. If everybody around you is not feeling particularly good but you're very happy and want to play the drums, you get yelled at. So you learn to hold back a lot of feelings. And then what you do is manufacture another layer.

In therapy I had to face the fact that I had hostile feelings. I couldn't believe that I had any hostile feelings at all. That was a surprise to me, but it was also very helpful. If a reviewer said anything bad about me in the newspaper, I would just feel hurt and sad—"Oh my goodness, how could he possibly say that about me?"—instead of being angry, which would have been OK.

I worked very hard for six months on a project, and somebody wrote: "Dom DeLuise didn't give that much thought." He was wrong. I was in Yugoslavia doing a picture—I left my family for six months—and worked *very* hard. But the critic said I didn't seem to give much thought. I was crushed at that. It would be healthier, it seems to me, to be angry and to say, "That shit."

In therapy I learned that it was OK to feel angry. At my wife, at my mother, at God, at the children, at the dog, at a baby. It's OK to feel angry. It doesn't mean you're no good. If you have that doubt in your mind that you are not in fact behaving from a basically good feeling, then when you *do* have a feeling coming up that is not so good, you suppress it so hard and strong that it knocks you off kilter. Does that make any sense to you?

My father yelled and screamed. I guess in order not to be like him when I was a kid, I tried to suppress anger. I guess I made a promise to myself that I'd never be like him, but I couldn't keep it, because every once in a while I would explode with anger. But I said, "I'm never going to be like papa; I'm not going to yell like that." Of course, that's a silly thing to lay on yourself when you're young, to say that you're not going to be angry.

My father frightened me, and I thought it was unfair of him. I get angry better that he did, though, because when I do it, my kids like me. They assume I'm angry, and then they know I'm going to be OK. And I'm cuter than my father was. I laugh more and I make up better. So I can have fights with my children and then tell them genuinely that I'm not angry anymore. And it's over very quickly.

He saved my life, my therapist. Don't omit that part! I was really very depressed, and I saw that therapy was really very helpful. It didn't take long to be very grateful to my therapist, although I loved him and hated him, respected him and had contempt for him. I went through all the emotions you go through when you have a therapist. And I was with him for about five or six years.

I was in an off-Broadway show in New York. I got some wonderful reviews—the *New York Times* said I was a comic genius—but then some other people didn't like my performance. Well, I mean I was completely crushed, and I didn't know what was going to happen. What happened was that I started not to function.

Usually if I'm upset, I eat. You can see I'm upset a lot, because I'm heavy. I'm a heavy person. It's very sad. But I was so upset that I wasn't even eating. I had no defenses. I was not suicidal, but I was crying all the time. I couldn't sleep, I didn't want to work, I wanted to be alone, and I became immobile. This went on for about a week, and it really frightened me, because it was the opposite of my nature. So I went to the doctor [therapist].

It took about three months, and there was a vast change in my behavior—in my attitude mostly—and I could see that I had been helped. I mean, it was very dramatic.

I was angry before at critics for having written not the nicest things about me, and I just felt sad and depressed instead of angry. Suppressing the anger clogged my works. Once I admitted I was angry, I could go on to the next step, which was to get over my anger and then get back to my joy. But there was so much anger—because it had to do with my career—and such a pulling-back of that anger. Now if somebody said something bad about me I could be furious—not necessarily with the person but certainly with his words—but I wouldn't have to call him up or write him a letter. I could know that I was handling my anger.

There were occasions when I told my therapist that he was an idiot, that he didn't know what the fuck he was doing, that I could see his technique, and that if he was trying to get me to cry or feel something, he should be a little more subtle. He should be ahead of me, not in back of me. If I could anticipate his every move, then he wasn't doing a good job, I thought. Or if he suggested something that I thought was wrong, I'd say, "You're wrong and that's silly." Even if I thought he was wrong in his technique, though, and said, "No, it's not that. Don't you see, it's that and that and that?" it was worth the fifty dollars an hour anyway, because you're finding out who the fuck you are and it's helping you think clearly.

There were days when I didn't want to go in. Then I would be late. And my therapist would say, "You're late, and it's going to cost you." I'd say, "That's fine; that's my business." And there were days when I tried to avoid the whole thing, sure. Sometimes it's wonderful, but you don't run to your therapist every time—or at least I didn't. Sometimes I didn't want to go because it was cold in New York, it was raining, or I felt happy. You know, sometimes when you're unhappy you run to the therapist faster. I mean, everything was going all right at the moment, and there was no eruption of emotion. Mostly I was functioning OK.

Once your doctor knows who you are, you don't have any secrets from him. I mean, he knows everything. You can be yourself with your doctor. He knew what I was about, my doctor.

I'm a comedian, and one of the first questions I asked my doctor was "If I get better, will I lose my sense of humor?" He laughed. And he said "No."

Sexuality is a subject that is genuinely suppressed, and therefore it's going to come out in the course of your therapy. I think it just comes up in conversation. In fact, there was a priest here at the house yesterday and *we* talked about sexuality. I like a lot of my sexuality. I think I'm very sexy. I don't mean sexy to other people but I mean I'm sex-minded. I think about sex all the time and I like affection a lot. We all run around naked and we talk about sex a lot. I like to discuss it—the first sex you've had, the last sex you've had—with my friends. I think it's fun. I like, in fact, to talk about the kind of sex my wife and I have—without being too literal. If we go away for the weekend, we discuss *if* we had sex. So I'm very open about it. I'm not a person who will hide his sexuality. It's funny: I don't seem to put a curb on sex, but I would like to put a curb on cupcakes and chocolate sandwiches.

I used to punish myself by overeating. I would like not to eat so much. I think that's my problem. I'm like an alcoholic when it comes to food. And I would change that if I could. I *will* change that. When you eat, I think what you're doing is suppressing a lot of feelings. So sometimes if I don't have food, I have a lot of feelings of panic. In order to suppress my panic, I have a little food.

I'm always talking about my childhood, even today with my children, with my wife and with my friends. In my nightclub act I talk about it. It always comes up. It's a strong part of my life. Holidays you remember it, and you try to duplicate some of the stuff that went on when you were a child.

What I'm going to say now may be a little strange, but I really feel that it's true. You already know when you go to a therapist what you need to know. You just talk it out with him. I don't think there's a subconscious that we don't know about. I think the subconscious is just underneath covers, and I think it's there for us to use. I don't think we're going to be shocked when we go to a therapist. I don't think the subconscious is that dark and deep.

You have to assume that there is a zestful child in you and in me—a happy, glad-to-be-alive human being. Something happens as you grow up that changes that. We may become someone who is the opposite of a happy creature. And it's not age that does it. I'm doing a picture with Mae West at the moment. She's eighty-four years old and she thinks of herself as a sex symbol, and she also thinks of herself as being young and pretty. She's amazing. She doesn't look eighty-four, but, more than that, she doesn't behave like an eighty-four-year-old. She hears everything with those wonderful ears. No matter what you say, it sounds like a dirty remark to her. She's sensational. And zestful. She has a great sense of humor.

My therapy was always ultimately pleasurable, even the crying, even the sadness. I mean, it was all very "for me." The overall feeling is enjoyment and pleasure that you are dealing with problems and settling them.

When something's over, it's over. When you leave your therapist you walk out, and you truly don't feel like "Oh my God, how am I going to function?" You just leave. It's not like ending a marriage, which makes you feel bad. You leave and it makes you feel good. Like when you leave your mother's house, when you're finally ready to get your own apartment.

You just go away. It's a nice feeling. You know, it's like you say, "I'll call you sometime. I appreciate your raising me and breast-feeding me and all that stuff. I'll see you around." And then you just leave. It's not torturous. You're happy to go because you have things to do.

Once when I was feeling very bad, I called my therapist in New York and said, "What should I do?" And he said, "Do what you like. Do something that gives you pleasure." So I went and I worked with wood. When I'm feeling bad I get right down to physical work.

I'd like to relax more; I'd like to have more chance to read. I want to answer my mail. But I don't want to be another person. I want to change a few things now but not a lot of things. I like to dance, I like to sing, I like to play, I like to swim, I like to make love—not necessarily in that order.

Dan Greenburg

Dan Greenburg is the author of *How to Be a Jewish Mother, How to Make Yourself Miserable,* and *Scoring* (described as "A Sexual Memoir") and is a frequent contributor to *Playboy* and other publications.

I was in Freudian analysis five days a week for about six and a half years. I got into it just after I arrived in New York about twelve years ago. I had suddenly found it impossible to eat with anybody—especially girls—without getting nauseous.

To this day I don't exactly know how this particular symptom came up. But it was very effective in doing its job, which was to prevent me from having to do with people. I would get so nauseous that, finally, even the *idea* of having dinner with anybody—specifically, ladies—was intolerable. I just stopped dating.

Obviously if you're going to have dinner with a young lady, then you're probably going to spend some time with her, and over a period of time you may have a romantic, a sexual relationship develop. I think in those days I was very ambivalent about both romance and sex. I had a very powerful pull toward these things and very great anxiety because of them.

Why? I can relate that to Freudian notions of mommies and daddies. To put it very simply, when you're a little boy and you're living with your parents, there's only one lady in the world and that's your mommy. And whatever sensual feelings you may have about her, it's very obvious that if you act on them and attempt to take her, your daddy is going to be very upset with you and—according to the Oedipal fantasy—kill you. Being killed as a very young boy is not an appealing prospect, so one represses one's sensual interests in mommy and, later, in any women in one's life who turn out to represent mommy.

So, when one has a close relationship with a woman and starts to have sexual feelings, there may be a trigger that says, "Wait a minute. Didn't we decide that acting out sexual feelings with ladies was dangerous?" This is not done on an adult level because the thought was conceived by a two-year-old or a three-year-old. And it remains kind of atrophied in that state.

Somebody I knew who was in therapy said, "Go to my therapist and he will refer you." It's lucky I got a good guy, because at that point I was so shy and so polite that I think I would have gone into therapy with Hitler, rather than say, "Listen, I don't think you're quite right for me."

When you're in therapy you assume that your therapist is, if not God, then certainly one of the heavenly host. And a heavenly host would have Catherine Deneuve or Charlotte Rampling for a wife. I remember once deciding that I didn't think my shrink's wife was as attractive as I thought she might be. (He had the sessions in his house, so from time to time one saw members of his family.) I was scared to tell him that. But I realized I was spending so much time thinking about it—like weeks of sessions during which I was thinking about nothing else—that I had to get it off my chest. I finally told him, and I'm sure he felt I was acting out anger against the analyst. In fact, that's probably what it was, but I was so out of touch with my feelings that I didn't know that. I mean, if I saw his wife today—now I'm not in therapy with him—I might think she was gorgeous.

One could characterize the relationship somewhat by the fact that, although I saw him five days a week for six and a half years, he called me Mr. Greenburg right up through the last day. I just somehow thought that on the last day he'd start calling me Dan, I'd start calling him David, we'd laugh about some of the old times, and I'd tell him his wife was really pretty good-looking after all. He'd say, "Boy, when you came in here, did the picture of a guy puking his guts out at the thought of having dinner with a lady make me laugh!" An arm around the shoulders, a little pinch on the cheek, and a "Hey, keep in touch, stay loose." *Something*! But there was nothing. It was just like a regular session.

I'm sure that that was his professional image, but it's hard to imagine that once he walked outside he suddenly put on dancing shoes, did a minstrel act, tap-danced down the street, and became Henny Youngman. I think that probably his social persona was not radically different from that which I experienced in the office. It's hard for me to envision him yocking it up, or having sex, for that matter. As a matter of fact, I think we discussed that for a while.

You can't shock these guys. I think I tested him at various points, dredging up incredible things I had done in my life and incredible fantasies I had about doing certain things. If he was ever shocked, he never indicated it. You could walk into one of these guys' offices and say, "Well, gee, I had a strange night last night. I met a Yorkshire Terrier in a bar and we went home, and had sex. Then three palomino ponies came over and we did it, too, and I think I may be in love with one of them." You'd get no reaction on that from most shrinks. They're professionally unshockable.

There's a terrific Bruce Jay Friedman short story about a guy who can't believe that his shrink will not be shocked or punitive about anything he tells him. And finally one day he announces to his shrink that he has just been to the shrink's house and murdered the shrink's wife. The shrink very professionally and impassively picks up the phone, makes one short call that establishes it's true, sheds just a couple of tears, and then becomes his professional self again.

After I had spent about six and a half years with my analyst, he announced that he was moving to New Jersey. I said, "What about me—do I move to New Jersey too?" And he said, "No, I think by the time I move we will have completed what we had to complete." (This was a few months prior to his moving.) And in fact we had done a lot. I was very quickly able to start eating with people again, even though I was not able to talk to them while I was eating. But I was not holding the retch back with my teeth, as was the case prior to Freudian therapy.

When this man left I had just gotten married or been married for a year or two. And then, a few years later, when my marriage [to writer Nora Ephron] started breaking up, I went to see a woman named Mildred Newman, whom I had actually met in the course of a project I was working on off-Broadway. I had sort of made a mental note at the time that if I ever needed therapy, I'd go see her. She's a brilliant woman and also very warm. I think at one time she was perhaps a Freudian, but now I guess she would classify herself as being eclectic.

I think what I get out of therapy with her is perhaps what was missing in the Freudian therapy with the other guy. In Freudian therapy one seems to be reinforced in a detached intellectual attitude toward one's problems and feelings. That played beautifully into what turns out to be one of my chief problems, which is that I'm somewhat detached from my feelings. It helps with being a journalist—which is one of the things I do for a living—but it really doesn't work too well for living a full life.

In Freudian therapy I found it very easy to reinforce my own unwillingness to deal with my feelings. Most anything I said was dealt with as an association and with the comments of either, "Well, what comes to mind about that?" or "Well, what do you think?" In all fairness to the man he did say other things, but I did hear those two phrases a lot more than I wanted to.

Anyway, two or three years after I stopped seeing this man, I began with Mildred. The main thing she concentrates on is getting one in touch with one's feelings. I go to her one day a week privately and one day a week in a group. I think this combination has produced a remarkable effect. For one thing, I'm able to be far more outgoing, far more confident and far more aggressive in social situations. I'm able to talk to people. Previously—despite all my therapy—I was unable at dinner parties and on TV talk shows to talk to more than one person at a time.

It was unthinkable to me that I could go to a dinner party and suddenly take the center of attention and hold it. As a result of group therapy, one of the things I've been able to do is precisely that. I've only been able to do this in the last year and a half, and the first time was an incredible moment for me. I was at a dinner party and doing my usual thing, which is to select one person to talk to. I was sort of aware that one guy at the table was holding forth and almost everybody was listening to him. What he was saying was on a subject I knew something about, the occult, on which I'd recently done a book after about three years of research. And what he was saying essentially was—though charming—entirely incorrect. And I thought, "Well, why don't I just point that out to him? What I have to say is equally interesting, if not more so." So I took the floor and told him he was wrong, and we had a very lively debate which went on for a couple of hours. And everybody sat enthralled. And I thought, "My God, I've actually been able to speak up in a group." And now I can do this at any time.

I did a show with David Susskind five or six years ago on Jewish mothers, based on a book I had written. I remember on that show there was a period of an entire hour during which I said nothing. That wouldn't happen again. In fact, it's becoming increasingly difficult to shut me up—which is a nice change.

I used to think that what I had to say was not interesting and nobody would want to hear it. Well, all that is utter nonsense, and I knew better intellectually even then. But emotionally I felt that I didn't have anything to say and that, even if I did, I couldn't say it entertainingly. I thought people would fall into instant slumber or start reading the back of their cigarette package or something. All that was before I got into group therapy, of course.

I'll tell you why I went into group therapy. First, because Mildred thought I ought to do it and I was humoring her. Second, because I thought, "Well, maybe it will make me better at dinner parties and on TV panel shows."

The first thing I noticed in group was that, when it got to be my turn, I really enjoyed talking about myself and my problems—and I really got a lot out of it. The second thing I found out was that other people weren't as boring when they talked about their own problems as I thought they'd be, because their problems were quite strikingly similar to my own. And the third thing I found out was that everybody in the group—except me, of course—had as a basis for their problems some incomplete relationship, when they were little, with one or both of their parents. After a while it sort of dawned on me that I was not the exception and that I too had problems arising from that basic relationship.

The next thing I discovered was that I was able to help people in the group with their problems, which was satisfying. And the next thing I found was that I was even willing to let *them* help *me*.

I'm preoccupied with sex, so a lot of my talk is about sex. It's probably no coincidence that my therapy group is known as the Mildred group that talks a lot about sex. It has that reputation.

In my Freudian analysis I think I was finally able to admit everything, however embarrassing, that I had ever done or thought on the subject of sex. There were things that I really would not have admitted to anybody but a psychiatrist—and even then it took quite some doing. And once I had told the shrink these things, they suddenly became totally tellable to anybody—in fact, I wrote a book about them, called *Scoring,* in which I tell almost everything I ever told my shrink.

At a certain point in therapy with Mildred a year or two ago, I said, "I'm finding it difficult to have any fantasies anymore." She said, "That's because you've lived them all out." And I think that's probably true. If you read *Playboy* at all, you'll know about a lot of those fantasies. But I guess I've also created new ones.

At times I'm utterly baffled that it is so difficult for me to get in touch with my feelings, and when I'm finally able to, it's still a new sensation. For instance, I've had a great difficulty in crying. I probably haven't cried more than an average of once every two years in my adult life—and it is not generally as a result of the things you'd expect to provoke tears. It's not sad or frightening experiences. It isn't even weddings that do it to me. It's curtain calls at a play in which the actors have done a good job and receive a tremendous ovation. I can feel tears spring to my eyes. This is an unusual response from somebody who has been as detached from his emotions as I.

In the past, a really stressful, emotional situation—like the breakup of a long-standing relationship—was seldom enough to produce tears in my eyes. And it isn't just the wonderful macho image that we've been saddled with, that says it's not manly to cry, which makes it so difficult. It's also not being in touch with how I feel at a given moment.

I just recently had quite a good session with my group and was able to cry for the first time in a couple of years. I think I got some of the rust out of the tear glands, because I just saw a kind of sappy, sentimental movie on TV the other night and boy, there came the old tears. So I think it was partly that that mechanism hadn't been working in a long time. And now, having used it once, it was possible to use it again. I dare not go to a play and experience curtain calls at this point—I'd probably flood the place.

I'm able to express anger now, which is an incredible release—and I think it's what's prevented me from getting stomach ulcers and a whole grab bag of other wonderful physical complaints. I think that since I've been able to get anger out I'm physically a lot healthier than I've ever been in my life.

Before, I was never able to get mad. My tack was to make my face an impassive mask and speak in this really measured, quiet voice. It's a maddening type of behavior and really quite hostile. When my marriage was breaking up, our arguments were characterized by my wife's being able to express a lot of anger and my dealing with it very detachedly and unemotionally, which got her even angrier.

I just blew up at somebody in a meeting today on a script for a pilot for a TV series I'm writing. Even there I let the anger go on longer than I should have, for about ten minutes. The instant I got mad at the guy, it cleared up the situation. I got the anger out, he stopped doing whatever bullshit number he was doing, and we were able to communicate like human beings.

I'm convinced that nobody is quite as in touch with his feelings as he might be or should be. Most people repress their emotions, but they've got to come out one way or another, and generally they come out in the form of physical ailments. It's better to let people know your feelings. Almost all people. Perhaps not people who have, say, submachine guns in their hands.

I co-wrote a book called *How to Make Yourself Miserable,* which has an entire compendium of the ways in which people do this. I'm quite aware of many of the things *I* do—but I continue to do them. For example, late coming. I've done this for forty years now. In fact, I even came late to my own birth: they had to induce labor. I always think of several things to do which delay my getting ready and several more things to do when it comes time to actually leave the house. So then I get to have a lot of anxiety en route, in a cab, running or whatever.

People who have never been in therapy consistently say in my presence things like "I would never go into therapy, because I certainly don't want anybody telling me what to do with my life." Well, very few therapists will tell you what to do with your life, or try to get you to change anything or stop doing anything. What they will try to do is show you that you have a choice—and enable you to have the choice. I have the choice, I think, of continuing to be late or not to be late. And I seem to have chosen, so far, to continue being late. At times I'm not late, and it's so striking that I congratulate myself and notice the reason that I've not been late. It's generally because being late would be a lot more self-destructive than I'm willing to be at this point in my life.

I'm told by Mildred that being late keeps me with my mother. I can relate to that by saying that when I was a little boy and was going to school, I would characteristically get up later than I should. My mother would nag me to get up and I would do so at a very leisurely pace. Even more leisurely would be the pace at which I would eat my food and get ready to leave the house. It used to drive my mother absolutely bananas. It was one of the few ways in which I could get a rise out of her. The most exciting part of our relationship was that I would be late and she would scream at me. It's not a terrific relationship to have with somebody, but it's better than nothing, and I thought the choice was nothing. So by perpetuating that pattern even in adult life—even when mommy lives in a different city—at some three-year-old level I'm still with her by continuing to come late.

There are still a couple of things left that I would like to accomplish in therapy: I would like to be able to come on time consistently, if it seemed appropriate to do so. I would like to have a little bit more of a choice about getting deeply involved romantically with some young lady and ultimately living with her, or something on that order. Although I was married for seven years, I must never have been totally comfortable in that situation. There was always some free-floating anxiety. I would like to be so free of that anxiety that if I wanted to live with a lady, I could. I don't know anymore whether I want to or not. I was fond of saying after I became divorced that I had been married and I had paid my debt to society and would never have to do that again. I was glad I was married—I benefited enormously from it—but I'm glad I'm not married now, and I've grown considerably since. It's very likely that I'll want to live with somebody again, and I hope I will have progressed far enough in my therapy to make that possible without any discomfort or pain. At the risk of being simplistic, I think that difficulty really has very much to do—again—with what we perhaps too quickly call the Oedipal situation. I think it is simply that we learn at a very young age and for a great many years that it is not appropriate to have sexual feelings about somebody of the opposite sex whom you are living with. And however old you get chronologically, it's difficult to totally discard that notion at the deepest level of emotion.

Although Mildred has been telling me about it for a couple of years, I never really took my detachment from my feelings seriously until a few weeks ago. I began to see then that almost all of my romantic relationships that ended unhappily directly related to the fact that I was not really there for the woman emotionally. It is, finally, very depressing to be with someone who is with you only physically. Most of the ladies went elsewhere to find somebody who was home emotionally—and I don't blame them. Hopefully that situation is coming to an end.

Two things were involved in helping me to see this. One was breaking up with one of the several girls I was going out with. The other was my group's deciding that it had had its fill of hearing about my many romantic entanglements. I thought it was in poor taste for them to be bored with hearing the same old story—with a different girl—every time. So we got into a little shouting. I was finally able to see that they were right for being bored with hearing essentially the same thing over and over again for four years. So I decided to try to look at my life and clean it up a bit.

I'm a lot happier with myself these days than I used to be. As a matter of fact, something that was said about me recently as a put-down was, I think, one of the finest compliments I've received in the past couple of years. I was with a date and we were to meet a man who characterized himself as a movie producer. Anybody can characterize himself as a movie producer. All it takes is the intent someday to produce a movie. Anyway, I was feeling very good about myself that night, having a lot of fun and being fairly flippant and outgoing. Toward the end of the evening my date said to this alleged producer, "Well, what do you think of Dan?" And he replied, "I'd say Dan has a crush on himself." I think *everybody* should have a crush on himself. Most people's tendency is to downgrade themselves, not to think very highly of themselves. So if I truly *could* get a crush on myself—and I'm working on it—I think I'd be home free.

Blake Edwards

The air conditioner was on full blast in Blake Edwards's office at Twentieth Century-Fox, and I began to look for some sign of frost on the windows. But the man who had directed *Days of Wine and Roses*, *Operation Petticoat*, *Breakfast at Tiffany's*, and *A Shot in the Dark* seemed oblivious to the frigid conditions.

Wearing tinted glasses, a blue print shirt open to mid-chest, a gold medallion, French jeans and colored sneakers, Blake Edwards was now enjoying the success *The Pink Panther Strikes Again*, the fourth "Panther" film which he has directed and co-authored.

He had responded almost immediately to my request for an interview, indicating when we met that he had strong convictions about what therapy can do for people. Except for one interruption (a call from his wife, Julie Andrews), Edwards spoke unhaltingly—and with feeling—about the problems that had led him to seek help.

The people I know very well who have gone through therapy went into it for the same reason I did. Things got so heavy that it became absolutely intolerable to exist. Having tried every other avenue of relief, cop-out, whatever you want to call it, there didn't seem to be anything left, any other alternative.

In my own case I just hurt so much and was in such fear that it was therapy or suicide. I don't intend to be overly dramatic, but in my case that was really the next step. At one point, actually, a very close friend stopped me from going off a roof. I don't recall the incident that well—it isn't that clear in my mind, so I can't positively state that I was going to destroy myself—but the way he depicts the incident, I was halfway over. Now maybe something unconsciously said, "He'll see me, he'll save me." It may have been some gesture to gain attention or say, "Hey, won't somebody help me?"

What was my problem? It was an entire life leading up to that point, a combination of things, a compounding of deep-seated problems that just began to grow and grow. It's too complicated—when you consider that I spent all of those years trying to just figure them out—to be able to sit down now and explain it simply.

I can be specific in somewhat general terms. I was a terrible hypochondriac. That was a symptom rather than a problem.

I got into drugs pretty heavily. When you're a real neurotic, to get into heavy drugs is a really bad trip. And particularly in those days when anybody who smoked grass was considered a dope fiend. It was a whole different cultural picture, so there was an enormous amount of paranoia connected with even things like marijuana. And there was enough paranoia in my life without drugs.

And there wasn't the concerted effort to understand and to put drugs into proper perspective, so that if anybody had a bad trip—as I did on mescaline one time—there was nobody around to give you a hand; there was no place to go where they would say, "Ah well, he's on a bad trip." It was really terrifying, because being in as much trouble as I was in emotionally anyway, the drugs just drove me further into it.

When I came out of the service I was in a lot of pain. I was hooked and I didn't realize it. I had gone into a naval hospital that had not been commissioned. A lot of us were in pain at that time, so it was much simpler just to go through the wards and give somebody a shot of morphine. So you began to manufacture more pain to get the shot.

I had a broken neck, broken back and multiple other injuries that gave me a lot of pain. I was able to kick the habit because I wasn't really that familiar with addiction at that point, and I didn't make the connection that much between all that morphine and the fact that I was so sick when I got out and was really kicking cold turkey.

I knew that I wanted morphine; I knew that I wanted something to relieve the pain, but I had no place to get it—I was too young. I complained to the doctors, and they gave me an empirin codeine or something like that, which helped. Then, eventually, I sort of smoothed out and there was no addiction, though in later years my injuries began to really kick up.

The psychic pains began to kick up too. Unconscious memory of the relief I got in the hospital came back to visit me in very strident terms, so I started on morphine again and went for quite a while. That was all a part of my eventual breakdown.

I actually kicked the habit before I got into therapy, which is a strange sort of thing, but it happened. I kicked the habit because I was blaming everything on the fact that I was hooked. Then, about a year later, I realized that my life wasn't getting better. All I was thinking about was a fix, and I was in terrible trouble. I was smoking a lot of grass, I was drinking, and I took mescaline one time, although I wasn't into any hard drugs again.

Madness was creeping up on me. I was frightened, in terror. I wasn't hallucinating or anything like that; I was just in the most profound depression and had the most terrible anxieties. I just felt that my life was in terrible shape. I couldn't understand why, and I tried everything to get out of it.

It was relationships with women, it was acting out, it was anything that gave me momentary escape and relief. Inevitably my relationships with women wouldn't work out. There would be deep jealousies, manipulations, and women who were mostly suicidal. I remember threats my mother used to make—locking the bathroom door, terrifying me that she was going to kill herself—and witnessing a suicide attempt she made at one point.

So I used to do a couple of things. I would get people—women mostly—and I would drive them to distraction, to the point of suicide, and then I would save them. I would surround myself with people who were cripples—creative cripples, emotional cripples. Even though they didn't seem that way on the outside, I knew instinctively that they would fail. Sooner or later they would fail me, and that was my protection. I didn't fail: they failed me. I had to deal with that, change it.

Eventually I complained to somebody—a man who happened to be in analysis—and he recognized what was happening to me and said, "Listen, I'll give you the name of my doctor." I went and talked to him but didn't like him, didn't feel comfortable. Obviously I didn't want to get into analysis, and I stayed away from it for almost another year.

Then it was so terrible—the nightmare of waking up every day in this deep depression. I went to New York and was having all kinds of personal problems with the lady I was involved with. When I got on the train to come home, there were three or four days of no sleep, of absolute terror, of thinking, "I'm going crazy, I *am* crazy"—that kind of thing. When I got off the train I had withdrawn almost completely, to the point where I couldn't talk. And the one thing that kept a kind of light at the end of the tunnel was that analyst I had seen. So I called him and told him I must see him. I told him quite frankly that I was disturbed and the reason I had left. He said he understood and suggested another man, the analyst with whom I eventually spent about five years.

I went into analysis when I was about twenty-eight or twenty-nine years old, which was around twenty-three years ago. The first three months were really spent just getting me around to the point where I could talk, where I could relate. I would go in day after day and just lie there while he would talk to me very quietly and almost put me into a state of hypnosis. He would just talk about relaxing so that I could eventually feel comfortable and secure enough to begin to talk to him.

At the beginning I was in analysis steadily for about three years. Then I began to move about in films and go on locations, which would mean being gone for three or four months. It was extremely difficult for me to be away from the analyst. If it had been in the beginning, I doubt I would have been able to do it.

The analyst was my complete savior, my last bastion, so I did everything I could do to convince myself and everybody around me that what I was doing was the best thing for everybody and that he was the greatest psychoanalyst who ever lived—all of those techniques that everybody resorts to in the beginning.

I continually felt that I was getting something out of my analysis, but there would be times when I felt I was sliding back terribly. Really what I was doing was coming up against closed doors, breaking down these closed doors and getting to the problem behind them. As I began to realize the dynamics of what I was doing, this became a little bit easier.

Even though I was always improving, sometimes I felt I was getting nowhere. I was saying to myself, "I've never been in so fucking much pain in my life." But you can't measure pain. As I began to realize that, I got a better perspective of what psychoanalysis was for me. As a result, when I got into those tough times and was *really* in trouble—even though I was in analysis—there was an element of reassurance, because I knew that that was the way it was supposed to be for me, that I was working through something. And I would fight all the harder to work through it so I could relieve myself—because I knew relief was at hand.

In the first year of my analysis there were very few days when I did not want to go. But later on there were days when I would feel really well and think, "I don't need it today." And that was the big struggle: to make myself go. I think I was going through a lot of the things everybody goes through in psychoanalysis, like fear of one's sexuality: "Am I homosexual, am I a heterosexual?"—all of those things that you have never truly examined for yourself.

You find yourself immediately talking about all the forbidden things that childhood made forbidden—and, obviously, the most profound part of that was sexuality.

The fears you have form a very complex mosaic. At one point there was the terrible fear that I really was a homosexual. I guess everybody goes through that in one way or another. And then you eventually turn around and say, "What's so bad about being a homosexual?" And then you dispense with that; you put it away. I am what I am. I recognize that I have parts of both. I've settled for a heterosexual life, and I'm very happy with it.

I think the biggest problem *was* my perspective of life and trying to be able eventually to reconcile that mine might not be an ordinary perspective. I think most of my life I had been afraid that I was different. On the one hand, I wanted to be different because it gave me a certain status: "I'm creative, so I'm different."

But deep down I was the child that most children are, who wants to be like his peers, who doesn't want to be different, who is afraid of difference. And so I had to deal with that. I suddenly realized that a lot of the things I saw and felt were not what a lot of people saw and felt—but that this was nothing to be terribly afraid of.

Nobody ever encouraged the creative side of my life, so therefore I was just afraid I was different. My parents really didn't encourage me, even though the evidence was there that I was headed undeniably toward something creative: that I was going to be a painter, a writer, an actor or something. My life was not particularly mixed up with reality. I dealt with fantasy more than anything else, because a great deal of my time was spent at an easel painting—which few other kids were doing. It frightened me a little bit, too, so I did all the other things the other kids did: I was a good athlete and all of that. So I wasn't that much different outwardly. But my insecurities as a human being made me a braggadocio and too loud and too determined. There was some identification as the odd man out.

During the first three years of my analysis, I think I had only one or two colds, whereas before I used to be constantly plagued with them—as I said, I was a tremendous hypochondriac. And my income quadrupled. I was prone to be superstitious about this, to think "I've had good luck." But that isn't it at all. Your head is just turned around. You're realizing your capacity—or close to it anyway—for the first time.

In those first three years it was as if there were a kind of magic taking place: I had found the magic potion; the analyst had the magic power. I hadn't gotten those superstitions out in the open and really looked at things in a completely logical way. I was getting relief, something I had never experienced before. Great! I was saved!

It hadn't bothered me that I was a hypochondriac, because I didn't recognize that I was. What bothered me was that I was sick all the time. Hypochondriasis is a very, very tough thing, because you make yourself sick. You can go to a doctor, and quite often he will say, "You're ill." If the internist had any experience in psychosomatic medicine, he could pick up on you pretty quickly. But in my case I had very real physical injuries, and if I was manifesting terrible pains, they would tend to be diagnosed as real. I could go in and complain and have somebody take care of me and love me—that's what it's all about. To cure really profound hypochondriasis is a very difficult thing, because the roots are complicated and deep. In fact, I don't think you ever completely get rid of it. I'm one hundred percent better than I ever was, but there are times when I do something to myself that I *know* is really hypochondriacal. Mostly it's in the area of back pains, and since the evidence is there of a previous physiological problem, the only way I can differentiate the real from the imagined is to stop and ask myself, "What kind of pressure am I under?"

I'm sure that in their way my family felt they were being very loving, but my requirements were such—because of many things that happened when I was really quite young—that I didn't feel that I was getting it—and I really wasn't. The child suddenly discovers that "Boy, when you're sick, you get a lot of attention." Attention was love. Get sick and get love. That's really oversimplifying, but there it is.

After about five years with my first analyst, I realized that there were a couple of areas that were just not resolving themselves, and I felt that if they weren't resolving themselves, then I wasn't with the right analyst. I had several conversations with my analyst about this problem, and he really felt that actually I had a good point: I wasn't helping me and he wasn't helping me to help myself. The areas in which I felt I wasn't getting help had to do with my former marriage—the fact that I was married, that it was not a good marriage, and that I wasn't dealing with it. And the analyst wasn't helping me.

My first analyst was a lay analyst. He asked if he could recommend someone else for me to see, but I told him I'd rather find the man myself. And I felt, "I'll shop around. What the hell. I'm not in any great pain, but I do recognize there are some things I want to clear up."

Well, the second man I found was an M.D. analyst. I was with him for about a year. At the end of this time he decided he didn't like L.A. and so he moved. And he sent me to another man, another lay analyst. And that was the best thing that ever happened to me, because the third man wisely said at that point, "I don't think the couch is where it's at with you anymore. I think you know that chapter and verse and are not really dealing now as you should with the problems that are important today." From then on was terrific.

I guess you finally deal with the hostilities you have toward your parents when you get certain things out in the open—like the fact that you really hated them at times, that their actions possibly gave you a wrong perspective about love and relationships. I remember the second analyst saying to me, "It's not enough now to recognize all those things; what are you going to do about them? You have now gotta say, 'OK, those things exist, but now I'm going to live my life.' You can't go on for the rest of your life saying, 'My parents didn't understand me; my parents didn't give me love.' " And you have to consciously do that.

How did my parents give me the wrong perspective about love and relationships? I'd be very hesitant to bring that up now, because they are alive, and it could be very unhappy for them. I had a father whom I never knew: I grew up with a stepfather. The image I got of my natural father was distorted, confused. I felt eventually that I had the bad seed and there was nothing I could do about it. The view that I was given of that missing parent—half of me, as I saw it—was that at times he was the devil incarnate. I would do something bad, and my mother would say, "That's your father; you are really your father's son." There would be other times when she would talk about him as the most handsome and wonderful man, obviously giving herself a lot of credit and remembering the romantic, wonderful thing that the relationship had been.

As I look back in retrospect, I think I must have said, "Hey, who is this guy who at one time—because things are not going well—is the devil, and the next moment is handsome, bright and intelligent?" I mean, that just fucked me up tremendously.

When I was forty years old I found him. I went to meet him. It didn't do much good; it just put one ghost to bed. He was just a guy. Actually now I look back and I love him. I'm a lot like he was. I wish he had had the benefit of an analyst. He would have done much better.

I've been with my third analyst off and on for fifteen years. He's a terribly bright man, and if I run into problems that I feel I want to talk out, I'll pick up the phone and call him. In my case, where I've had a lot of domestic problems with kids and things like that and want to be sure that I deal with them as well as I possibly can—I'll consult my analyst. He's been enormously helpful with my kids, my life, my marriage.

If communications between Julie [Andrews] and me start breaking down, we recognize it immediately, and we do something about it. There's dialogue. We say, "What the hell is going on? What are we being so gritty for?" We investigate. We think too much of ourselves and each other to allow that kind of existence to continue. Our personal happiness is too important. If we find out that maybe it's something a little too complicated that we can't solve, we pick up the phone and call my analyst or she'll call hers.

It happens particularly when we are dealing with the problems of our family, our children, because I have my children from one marriage, she has her child from another marriage—a situation that always creates a problem—and we have two adopted kids. So you've got to keep all those balls in the air and have time to enjoy each other and still be good parents.

Sure, there are extra pressures because we are both in show business, but I would say we probably manage it better than most, because we both have examined it and looked at our priorities. She has admitted that her need to succeed at this point—her need to go on and be an actress-singer—is not as important as my need to continue my career. She is happy being a mom; she is happy writing now. She would like to continue to one degree or another—to do concerts occasionally, to do a week at Vegas, not to stop entirely—and I know her decision is not designed so that she will be a martyr.

We work our lives so that we are seldom apart. If she's got something to do, I try to manage so that I'm free and can be in charge of the family. When she did a year of television, I just wrote and was with the kids. We were in completely reversed roles, which was an interesting experiment for both of us. It was very helpful.

I remember in the beginning, when we met, suddenly I was directing not only my leading lady but the woman I was in love with, and she was doing love scenes with other guys. I thought I was a terribly sophisticated, psychoanalytically oriented fellow, but I found out I was getting jealous and being a complete, utter shit because of it. Had I not been analyzed—had she not been analyzed—I don't know where that would have led.

I'm the same person essentially that I was in the beginning; it's just that now I have the equipment to deal with my problems. But I'm still tempestuous; I still become very black and terrifying in order to win arguments. I intimidate, but I know it, and I stop myself much more quickly. My temper is the main thing that people find the most difficult about me. That flaring. Because I'm like an animal. My kids—the little ones—respond to it more than the older ones. My wife just says "Bullshit" and doesn't put up with it. Because she knows it's a conditioned thing: I had to win, had to prove that my perspective was right because I was so terribly afraid it wasn't.

I am totally imperfect; I make all kinds of mistakes; I fuck up constantly. I get concerned with my fuck-ups, but my concern is not as great as before. I am infinitely more tolerant about myself and consequently infinitely more tolerant about other people and my family.

I still have a fear of dying. Well, who the hell doesn't? I'm sure that when my time comes, I'll revert to all kinds of superstitious nonsense, but I really won't until my time comes.

I want to be happy and I try to be happy. I want to be healthy and I try to be healthy—I do as much as I can. Beyond that, I work very hard to be successful, because I find my work is really good for me. It's very much like therapy, particularly the writing, because I do write out a lot of my demons. If something really gets to be pretty heavy, I can turn it around and make fun of it at a certain point.

I don't worry about success now. I worry about work. I want my work to be good, because that guarantees that I'll be able to get other jobs. It's the doing that I derive gratification from.

I still have a long way to go. I still clutter up my life with too many people. I still have a big need to take care of people, to do what I felt wasn't done for me—all of that, but I recognize it and I minimize it. I'm doing better. I imagine that by the time I do have to face my ultimate demise, I'll look back and say, "Shit, I'm just now getting on to it; I've just now made it." But that's better than not.

Trish Van Devere

Trish Van Devere has appeared in such motion pictures as *One Is a Lonely Number, Where's Poppa?* and *The Savage Is Loose.* On Broadway she co-starred with her husband, George C. Scott, in *Sly Fox.* She also appeared opposite Scott in the television special *Beauty and the Beast.*

I think your book is a good idea because, at this particular time, there are still people with young kids who have an attitude that steers them away from therapy. They think it's some reflection on them if their kids need some kind of counseling. Your book, I think, could be a big help toward getting rid of that kind of taboo.

I have worked with as a patient and known for a number of years Dr. Samuel T. Shine of Teaneck, New Jersey. He works a lot with children and has this problem with many parents' attitudes about a kid needing counsel. And in this day—with the kind of values we're consistently bombarded with on television and in life in general—I don't see how anyone can escape needing some sort of counsel.

I first went into therapy when I was in my early twenties. I simply wasn't functioning. I mean, to an extreme degree. I have a tendency to be a depressive. I'll have several very black, in-the-pit kind of days, and then I'll be up and all right. I know it will go away. But during that particular time, it was very bad. At that time I guess it was the worst it's ever been, and I was simply going to bed, staying in bed for literally weeks on end and practically not getting up. And so I said to myself, "Wait a minute, there's something wrong here."

So I went through some tests with a team of people, one a psychiatrist and one a psychologist. The psychiatrist—who will remain nameless—had the kind of personality that drove me right up the wall. He was kind of hysterical, and everything was terribly disorganized. He had his office in his house, and there were kids running all over the place. I thought, "Well, my goodness, if they tell me he's the one I have to stay with, forget it!" As it turned out, he was not. But his partner has absolutely the opposite personality, the kind of personality that fits me very well. His approach is that "There's nothing that can't be handled; it's not the end of the world." It's just coping with the situation. He never gets upset, never gets excited—and that's what I needed for reassurance. I need somebody who says, "Everything is going to be all right. Now we'll just discuss this; there's a way of solving it." That, to me, is extraordinarily helpful and necessary. So I've stayed with him for a number of years, and now I go back to see him whenever I'm on the East Coast.

I feel that after a certain age all they can do—any of them, including the very best—is patchwork, because I think it's much earlier that the damage you're going to carry around with you is done. And that's why I think it's so important that psychology be in the grammar schools as a regular program. This way children very early on learn to air their frustrations and fears in a common group and find out they're not such freaks: that other people have these kinds of feelings of inadequacy that we all suffer from. Little ones, especially, don't realize that maybe the brightest, prettiest girl in the class or the biggest, strongest, smartest boy has problems, too. It's generally a reassuring thing.

By the time you get a lot older, so many of your damaging habits are already formed that it takes a lot more work and more conscious effort to overcome the obstacles you set up for yourself. And sometimes you can't see that you're setting up these obstacles because you're doing it in a way with such finesse. That's when it's necessary to talk to somebody who can see what you're doing as you speak about it.

When I was on the West Coast for a few months, I saw a Gestalt therapist, which was very different. Dr. Shine combines Freud and a very practical day-to-day approach. He uses your background, your childhood, to go back and show you the kind of repetitious obstacles you are using now—referrals back that you no longer need because they had to do with you as a child and your problems *then*. The Gestalt therapist, on the other hand, doesn't want to know about your background. He wants to know the here and now, how you're feeling, what you're doing, what's the matter, what you want to change. He puts it in your hands. If you want to change something, *you* change it—and you're the only one who can. In other words, it's giving back the power to you instead of forever giving it away to somebody else—that is, blaming somebody for your problems. I think both types of therapy are very valid and necessary, but which is more suitable depends on the individual. I find them both helpful.

My father died when I was nine. I had a very domineering mother, and she took over the household. She was a person who tended to have a great deal of anxiety plus a great deal of energy. To her, if everything wasn't perfect, if everything wasn't right, you could not envision how terrible this was. It truly *was* the end of the world. Finally that anxiety and pressure and perfectionism become so introjected that you find yourself doing exactly what you hated your mother for doing. You have it within yourself. And you have to be aware when it's becoming operative and when it's really messing you up. I think that if you're with a therapist you can more readily see it.

You realize that all you do is dwell on your inadequacies and the things you've done wrong. You never ever see the other side of it: the things you have given that have been good. Dr. Shine is the one who has been able to point it out to me, especially in circumstances where it's simply inappropriate behavior. He's been very helpful as far as that insight's concerned. Sometimes you get such blinders on that you can't see anything except one narrow path, and it becomes enough to drive you batty. When that happens, I'll get so down on myself that I won't do anything. Then, slowly but surely, I climb out of the pit and I come back. It's a repetitious process and one that it seems can't be broken.

If I was going to be late or couldn't keep an appointment, I would be in such a condition, I'd call him hysterically. This was maybe twelve years ago. He'd say, "Trish, it's all right. If you can't come at four-thirty, I'll see you at five-thirty, that's all." And I'd say, "Oh, it's that easy?" In other words, any imperfection or mistake was so monumental in my eyes that I could never see that it could be solved that easily—with his never yelling at me or being angry with me. He calmed me, he quieted me, until we could look at things in a more detached, relaxed way.

I always felt as though I should be functioning and producing at a much greater level than I was, and I think that's something that stays with me today. I can't get over it. No matter how much I do it's not enough; I must do more. I think it is instilled when you're very young. I guess with some people it can be broken, but I think it's a vicious thing that, for the most part, you carry with you forever. It drives me crazy if I'm feeling that I'm operating on two cylinders when I really need to be operating on twelve cylinders. I don't know if I could ever satisfy myself and say, "You know, you're really functioning very well here." Most of the time I'm very dissatisfied with my work. Every once in a while—maybe in *One Is a Lonely Number,* maybe in *Where's Poppa?*—I say, "Well, OK, I don't think I could have done that any better. I think I did the best job I could do." That's as much as I ever give myself. But the rewards for me always do come from work. I'm a very work-oriented person. I'm not a recreation person, and I don't direct my energies to anything that seems sideline to me. This is something that both Resnick [the Gestalt therapist] and Shine have pointed out to me. They've said, "You're missing a lot of life by not enjoying other things."

How I feel I'm doing in my work determines how much I feel I've earned or am entitled to, and then that will reflect itself in how relaxed I am in a personal situation. In other words, if I'm feeling good about myself—and this always comes from feeling good about my work—then I'll relate well to other people. If I feel I've let myself down, then that distorts my relations with other people. Because then I'm operating out of "the little girl feels bad" or "the bad little girl," as opposed to the grown woman who's done a job and feels in control and generous and good enough about herself. When I'm feeling good about myself, I tend to be much more generous, giving, alive and outgoing.

I have a tendency always to look upon my weaknesses and my fallibilities. It used to be that I wouldn't go to an interview for a job because I didn't think I was attractive enough or talented enough. I'd think of something and I'd come down with some psychosomatic illness so that I couldn't go to the interview. Just out of fear of rejection. And so what I would do is reject myself first and not give anybody else the chance to reject me. And then, of course, I'd crucify myself for having done that. And then I'd be in the pits and have to call Dr. Shine.

My self-image was very bad. I had just a very bleak outlook on things in general. I thought I was inadequate. My feeling was that I was never going to shape up, never be able to satisfy myself no matter what I did, so why even bother? I think I've shrugged quite a bit of that off—not nearly as much as I'd like to, but it's gotten a lot better.

When my father died when I was nine, he had been ill for a while. More than anything on earth I wanted him to get better and come back to me. And when he didn't, I think that did something very damaging. I don't know how you can ever brace a child against something like that, but I often think the crisis is never as permanently damaging as how it is dealt with. I guess mine was not dealt with well at the time. And I developed terrible angers, angers against the world. I stopped believing in God, stopped believing in a lot of things. I expected never to get what I wanted, because what I had wanted most, I guess, in all my life, was that my father would get better. And he didn't; he died. Nine years old is just a little too young to cope with that. So I guess it remains an unfinished relationship whereby, in some sense, you're always seeking a father, a father figure, looking for your adoring daddy. Whether you realize it or not, you're doing it, even after he's been dead for twenty some-odd years.

My anger zeroed in on my mother. I felt that I could have taken better care of my father. I mean, there was some kind of childlike thought like that. I blamed her, in a way, for the loss of him. It's been asked if I had any anger toward him for leaving me, but I don't think I did. The anger went someplace else. He ever remained the perfect untarnished ideal.

He was an older man when I was born, and I was his first child and his only daughter. He and I were very close. I mean, I didn't even want my mother in the situation. And then, I guess, later on I felt guilts about that. I think I realized by the time I was about thirteen that somewhere deeply I had harbored the wish that it had been she who had died and not he. I just always wanted it to be daddy and me. And he wasn't there. So I felt very abandoned and alone.

When I first went to see Dr. Shine I was so glad to have found somebody like him and to have found *him* in particular. I used to have terrible anxieties that something would happen to him, that he would die or be in a car accident. I think that's sort of an attitude that I hold: that whatever I have, it might go away; I might lose it. Obviously that was the fear, the carry-over, from having lost my father.

Therapy is a very individual thing, and I think one should know, if they are going to seek some counseling, that they must have a rapport with the therapist. And if they don't, it's not going to work. Psychiatry is as good as the psychiatrist and as good as the way you relate to him.

I responded to Dr. Shine immediately. Our relationship has always been kept on an absolutely professional level, but it has been warm, empathetic and respectful. It has always maintained its objectivity. I've known him twelve years and he's still Dr. Shine to me. I never had extreme feelings toward him. He was always the safe person and place. I didn't harbor hostility toward him in any way, nor did I go through any kind of falling-in-love-with-your-psychiatrist bit. I never did that at all.

You don't want to go to the therapist on days when you're really feeling down, really feeling bad, really feeling low on yourself. Nothing seems to have any merit or worth, and there's no point in doing anything about it—it's just all so dark and gloomy and awful. These are the times when you should force yourself the most to go, and these are the times when sometimes you don't go.

If you approach therapy intelligently, you're supposed to take away from it a certain amount of strength and self-functioning—and not a dependency on it. If you're not doing the work in some kind of disciplined way and taking away from therapy what you should, a dependency can develop. But still it's a more honest kind of dependency than others which you might go into to avoid facing yourself or facing pain and conflict.

Sammy Cahn

"If you could buy the Academy Award, I would have bought all of them," Sammy Cahn is once reported to have said. Although the honor is not up for sale, Cahn has done rather well. The study of his house in Beverly Hills contains four familiar-looking gold-plated statuettes and more than twenty framed Oscar nominations. Several gold records, framed letters from Senator John F. Kennedy and Princess Margaret, and a photograph of Cahn with Betty Ford at the White House are among other memorabilia on view.

I had found my way into the room with a little help from the songwriter's striking wife Tita. "Just follow the sound of the typewriter and you'll find Sammy," she had advised.

The short, bespectacled Cahn—whose lyrics have helped make classics of such tunes as "Call Me Irresponsible," "All the Way," "Come Fly with Me," "Love and Marriage," "High Hopes," "My Kind of Town" and "The September of My Years"—was attired in a yellow terry cloth shirt, yellow pants and black loafers. Our conversation was occasionally preempted by the ringing of the phone at his side; an attached amplifier brought the voices of his callers—such as director Mervyn LeRoy—booming into the room. After each call, Cahn would resume his methodical account of his encounters with therapy.

Around 1963, when my marriage was in trouble and my wife and I were separated, I was asked to go into therapy. I consider myself a reasonable human being so I said, "Of course." I intimidated my wife's analyst, Dr. Judd Marmor, into taking me on as well. I understand there is some rule about an analyst not having both a man and a wife as patients—I guess a marriage counselor handles that type of situation. Anyway, Dr. Marmor agreed to see me as well as my wife.

A fetish of mine was that I just didn't like the notion of lying on a couch. To use a show business term, I thought it was corny. It seemed like something out of too many B movies I had seen. So I said, "I'd be much more comfortable, if you don't mind, if I could just sit and talk with you." So he said, "Fine," and that's the way we proceeded.

His first line to me was "Who are you to tell your wife she can't hate her mother?" I found it very funny, because I do not at all subscribe to the mother-hate scene. I don't understand it, I really don't. Maybe it's another time or another way of life, but I just didn't understand it. I think I am, in a great sense, a total purist and a total product of a certain life-style. I believe that your mother doesn't wake up in the morning and say, "What can I do to ruin my son's life?" Whatever she does is something she needs to do and does in your interest. Whether that well-intentioned scheme of things works, I'm not sure. But I cannot, to this moment, fault my mother for anything, because she did what she needed to do, which was probably the result of an upbringing by a mother who did what she had to do—and it goes on and on.

I just know that when I was punished, I had been bad. I admired my mother to a great extent, really admired her. She came from the most incredibly humble background and made it to America. Think of what courage it took to come to a foreign land without money, without knowledge of the language or the customs! You gotta like somebody just for doing that.

My point is that if you've grown up and you're matured, why do you want to worry about your mother?—unless you're looking for some scapegoat.

So one of the big problems in my marriage to my ex-wife was that she felt this terrible antipathy toward her mother. I *liked* her mother. I'll never forget that every time the phone would ring in the evening and the maid would come in and say, "It's your mother," my wife would grimace, raise her eyes to the heavens and say, "My God, it's her again." And I thought this was having a terrible effect on our children. I thought, "If they see *their* mother do it, one day she's going to call them and they'll do the same thing. I know it." So I just debated with that all the time. My own mother had great control over my family and was greatly beloved by my family. I had four sisters and they were all absolutely and totally respectful and dedicated to my mother. She earned our respect and love. Now perhaps my ex-wife's mother didn't deserve or earn it, but I didn't know what was to be gained by such antipathy.

"Who am I to tell her not to hate her mother?" I said to Dr. Marmor. "I'll tell you who I am—I'm her husband." I said, "I have a father who is very, very old and in a nursing home, and every day one of my sisters goes to comfort and care for him." I said, "Children who see that would benefit from it." Hate begets hate, and love begets love. I really believe that.

I went to see Dr. Marmor completely devoid of any preconceived attitudes or feelings, because, you know, I still don't know exactly what it is that therapy does. I just chatted with the man. He angered me a great deal. I was opposed to everything he advocated—terrifyingly opposed. I will admit that when I went away and thought about what he had said, I conceded that it was perhaps worthy of a try. And eventually I did everything he said to do. But I didn't concur.

I wish I could say that he was absolutely right and it had a happy ending, but there was no happy ending. All the king's horses and all the king's men could never have put the marriage together again. Perhaps analysts do a service by breaking up marriages.

The analyst told me I should move out of my home to a place nearby. It was easy for him to advocate that, but to me my home was my absolute life. I'd built this home, I'd watched every nail go into this home, and I didn't see why I should leave everything in the world that I loved because the lady had become disenchanted. Why didn't *she* leave? But he asked me to do this. He asked me to leave Camelot and live on the outskirts of it. And I did.

One day I came into his office and my wife was sitting there. I thought I had made a mistake, but he assured me I hadn't. He said he wanted me to go home, to my home. I told him, "I don't want *you* to tell me to go home, I want *her* to tell me to go home." And he said—I thought incorrectly—"That's the trouble with you. I wouldn't ask you to go home if she didn't want you to go home." But I think he was wrong. She should have said, "Darling, I want you to come home." Quietly, to me alone. "Take my hand and take me home." You don't have a relationship through a third party. I don't believe you do.

My wife had gone through a series of these psychosomatic ailments. She woke up one morning and couldn't move her arm. She went through all kinds of tests and discovered there was nothing wrong with her arm. Then she had these terrible headaches. They were such headaches that we thought it had to be a tumor in the brain. But of course it was nothing.

I saw the marriage disintegrating with this series of things. I had begun to try to save this marriage by making myself absent. I went on trips I didn't have to go on and I sent her on trips by herself. But nothing would help. So finally I said, "There's nothing wrong with you; the doctors say you're absolutely physically perfect." "So what are you trying to tell me," she asked, "—that I'm crazy?" "I'm not trying to tell you anything. But I'm saying that a doctor per se is not the answer." So she started to go to a therapist.

My divorce was really a cruel blow to me. It was one of the cruel, cruel things that happened in my life. And I tried desperately to ride over it and pass through it, but it kept becoming more and more oppressive. So I called my business manager, Eddie Traubner—as I do when I'm in times of great, great stress—and I said, "I just can't handle it."

I think when you get to a point in your life where you can't handle it, you must seek whatever help you can get. You go if someone says go see a witch doctor or go see this man who paints white paint on the top of your head and talks to you in a mumbo-jumbo—whatever it is, you must do it.

At Eddie Traubner's suggestion I went to see this Reichian therapist in New York. I was meeting this doctor surreptitiously because he wasn't allowed to practice in New York. He said, "You're angry." And I said, "I'm so angry I could die." He asked, "Did you ever hit that lady?" I said, "I've never hit anyone in my life"—and I never have. I've never struck anyone in anger. As a matter of fact, I have a recurring dream—I should go to an analyst for this—in which I really try to hit someone, strike him. But I feel like my arms are paralyzed; I just can't do it.

Anyway, the doctor asked me if I'd lie down on the couch on my stomach. He asked me to hit the couch, so I did. I started to hit the couch and I started to cry. And he asked me what I was crying for. I said, "I'm crying because Sammy Cahn, at age fifty, is lying here and hitting this couch."

I haven't gone back to my wife—I don't think you can go back to a relationship. To this day I don't talk to my ex-wife, because I don't believe she behaved decently. On a personal basis I don't speak to her because she hurt me. But that's OK. I do a kind of personal analysis of it. I said if my wife had ever come to me and said, "Look, I don't love you, but I'd rather die than hurt you—but that's it with us," what could I say? But it never happened that way. I was just let down by a series of cruel hurts, as I saw it. And one day I couldn't stand it anymore and I walked away. It may be a quirk in my character, but, above all else, to thine own self be true. And when someone says, "I don't love you, I don't want you"—by whatever means—OK, goodbye. But you can't have it both ways.

You know, a songwriter has a curious penalty to pay at the end of a love affair. He's haunted by all his songs. Wherever he goes, he hears his songs. And these are songs that sing of better times. I wrote all the love songs that were supposed to make for great happiness. "Love and marriage, love and marriage/Go together like a horse and carriage"—they don't seem to. "When somebody loves you/It's no good unless he loves you/All the way." It didn't go all the way. And the community property law in California is especially painful to a songwriter, because, although I am divorced and my ex-wife is remarried and has a child by her new husband, I am still obliged to give her half the royalties on all the songs I wrote during our marriage—to this moment. Not only do I hear the songs, but I hear them and know they're costing me money. I'm able to laugh at it now, but it's not a pleasant thing. If a man wants out of a marriage, he should give whatever he needs to give to get out. But if a woman wants out, she should walk away. She shouldn't penalize a man for the happiness she feels she wants. *She* should pay the price.

It's funny, my next involvement with analysis was through a third party. There was this girl I was seeing. I couldn't see any happy ending to our relationship, so I stopped seeing her. One day she called me and said she must see me one more time. I said, "I don't see why you want to resume this tasteless relationship." But she insisted. So I went to see her and she said to me, "It will please you to know that you've driven me back to my analyst." And I said, "I did?" And she said, "Would you like to know what the analyst thinks of you?" "Thinks of me?" "Yes, this is a lady analyst. And she says that you are a dirty lollipop." I started to laugh, because I realized immediately that it was the perfect title for a comedy play. I and a young chap called Jeff Burkhart then wrote a play called *The Dirty Lollipop.* Anyway, this girl I had dated said her analyst said she was a little girl who had dropped her lollipop in the dirt and was trying to salvage it, and the best thing to do would be to just toss it away—and I was the dirty lollipop.

I've never met an analyst who I didn't think needed analysis. I guess listening to all that stuff must have an effect. I'm not sure.

I think analysts can also become a terrible crutch, which most of them do. I don't like to sound negative about it, but I have negative attitudes because I don't quite understand what the service is. I know what the service is supposed to be, but I don't know what the clinical proof of it is.

I had one other experience with therapy. Into my second marriage a curious thing started to happen. My life-style normally is absolutely, totally involved. Not a day goes by that I don't do some kind of creative work. Right after my second marriage, for some curious reason, I got into this slump. It was so strange. Here I was married to this young, beautiful lady—a really marvelous girl named Tita—and all of a sudden I was in a slump. The phone wasn't ringing. Everything stopped.

I couldn't acclimatize myself to this new set of circumstances, and I found myself suddenly getting uptight to the point where I felt I couldn't live inside myself. My skin was closing in on me. I tried to counsel myself, but finally I went to my wife and said, "I must tell you something. I think I'm going out of my mind." So she said, "Why don't you go see a therapist?" She, funny enough, sent me to see a fellow called Arnold Hutschnecker. He has the dubious distinction of having been Nixon's analyst. This Dr. Hutschnecker wrote a book called *The Will to Live.* And I believe in lots of the theory of the book, the point being that we decide when we die. The book is based on a quote from a letter that George Bernard Shaw wrote. He said in this letter that he was ninety-some-odd years old and had lost the will to live. And very shortly thereafter he died.

Anyway, my wife had a friend who was going to see Dr. Hutschnecker, and she asked if he'd see me. So I went again, this time in New York. He said what I was going through was a very normal period of down cycle or stress. He gave me a little pill. I couldn't understand how anything that tiny knew what it was supposed to do or how it got to where it was going to do what it was supposed to do. But these pills—combined with a sugar-tolerance test later and a subsequent new diet—helped me.

I had wanted this beautiful young girl whom I'd married to experience some of the life-style I was accustomed to. And very shortly thereafter a series of events happened which kind of brought me back into a whole new career. I went on the

Broadway stage, we did a show in London, we've traveled, and life has been as exciting as ever.

I've written songs with five or six different men, and every time we've parted it becomes very traumatic. When you've been writing with a certain man for years and years, it's almost like a marriage ending. The two of you become one, and every song you write is almost like having a baby. You get involved in a life-style and relationship that's very intimate and very, very demanding—again, almost like being married. Before my second marriage I had just parted with Mr. Jimmy Van Heusen rather amicably. It was an incredibly fallow period, although it hasn't been fallow since. Funny enough, this past year has been for me one of the most incredibly important years. I went out on the road again with my show, I just finished the score for the first musical version of *Heidi,* etc., etc. This year has been the most productive year of my life, and I was sixty-four on June 18.

I'm a true believer that life isn't sunshine and flowers and the birds singing every day. Life is imperfect, which makes it perfect.

I had a traumatic experience with both my children. My son I didn't talk to for a long time. My daughter and I are kind of estranged, but amicably now. But, you see, I have a very simple rule about that as well. They don't have to like me, but, likewise, I don't have to like them. If they're nice to me, I'm nice to them. If they're not nice to me, fine. It's like a friendship. If people behave badly to you, you don't let them in your house; you don't associate with them. So why associate with your children if they treat you badly? I was as good a father as I knew how to be. If I failed, I failed from stupidity but not from a lack of love. And I'm sure they know I love them. If they need me, I'll be there.

I have a kind of stone-age attitude about therapy. I know it must do a great, great deal of good, because if it didn't, why would so many people be into it? But I do a great deal of *self*-analysis. I talk to myself, I berate myself, and I chide myself. I give myself points when I'm decent and I also give myself demerits when I'm not. I just never, ever quite got into therapy for some reason. I can live with myself. I find myself a decent person. I try to do a kindness every day. If I came to a point, though, where I felt my skin closing in, I would see whatever doctor anybody would suggest, because I don't know what the alternatives are.

Janis Ian

Janis Ian was annoyed. Her Hollywood hotel room was cold—no manipulations of the thermostat could coax any warm air from the vents—and the same thing had happened earlier in another of the endless string of rooms she occupies while on tour.

Diminutive and wiry-haired, Ian has been fighting small battles—and describing them in affecting songs with universal appeal—since her youth. She was a pop star at fifteen with a hit called "Society's Child" but was absent from the music scene for years thereafter. More recently, "At Seventeen" and other successful recordings have returned her to a position of eminence among the small corps of female singer-composers.

With a musician's concern for equipment, Ian checked out my tape recorder before we began. Then, sipping a glass of white wine, she discussed "the very important part" that psychotherapy has played in her life and work.

When I was about sixteen and a half I was crazy. I was doing a lot of drugs, very entranced with the romantic notion of the artist as an incompetent. There's a lot of mystique to being crazy. It was terrific, those first four or five months that I was really full-blown crazy. I was being very artistic: there I was with my hash pipe and wine, and I was creating. It was great while it lasted, but it gets frightening when you can't stop it. You make yourself hallucinate to fulfill the expectations. I used to hallucinate cellos because I love the cello. And then I couldn't stop it. That's really scary.

I had, I guess, what you could call a nervous breakdown for about a week. It should have lasted about a day. Someone—my parents, I think—took me to a shrink—one of those guys who gets his Ph.D. for being snotty. Anyway, he put me on something called Stelazine. I overreact to drugs anyway, and he didn't tell me that it had a cumulative effect. So they left me on it for about a week, and at the end of the week I couldn't even talk. It had a very heavy-duty cumulative effect. It was like a horse tranquilizer.

My friends took me down to a shrink they knew in Philadelphia. He took one look at me, said "Oh, shit," gave me a shot, and I was fine. But I decided I needed some kind of help. I needed somebody to talk to me who didn't want me to be a star or a lover or anything. Someone who could be a friend if I really needed one but who was not going to judge me.

The first man I had seen was a psychiatrist. This other guy, in Philadelphia, is a psychologist. I saw him for about two years pretty intensively and then another year not so intensively. We would always have long gaps between sessions because one or the other of us was going away. I might see him three times in one week and then not see him for two weeks. It was pretty loose and unstructured.

He didn't make me come to his office, because when I did, everybody else there would get strange: they had a star to show off in front of. So we'd talk at his house.

I really wanted somebody who knew some answers because I had none. At that point I was so screwed up that I didn't even know what questions to ask. And Gerry (the therapist) understood that.

If I hadn't been a star I probably wouldn't have had the money to see a shrink, but I don't think it [the stardom] would have made any difference to my basic personality, which was just in need of some adjusting. I was always real bright when I was a kid, a lot brighter than everybody else around me, and able to fool everybody around me whenever I wanted to. I was just not dealing with reality.

The main thing with therapy, I think, is to happen on the right person, the right method for you. And I got lucky, you know. I sat down with that cat and he read me in ten minutes. He knew I was bullshitting. I knew I was bullshitting. But he was the first person who had the balls to say it. He had nothing to lose.

I knew I was almost all facade, but I didn't know what to do about getting rid of it. The real me was always masked. I was revealing myself in a very calculated way. I mean, everybody's got their little rehearsed stories. I had just not dealt with myself in a long time. I discovered that if I was going to be a writer, I could either lie all the time or be honest all the time. But I'm not one of those people who can do both: I can't go on stage and bullshit and then come off and be real. I have to be real all the time.

I had grown up with the attitude from my parents that people who saw shrinks were always crazy and my seeing one was, almost of necessity, embarrassing to them. But after about two weeks I just felt so relieved that I didn't care who knew—and I still don't, really. It was a very important part of my life. When you sit down and talk to anyone—it doesn't have to be a therapist: it can be anybody you trust—just the act of talking relieves you.

I find that if I don't verbalize things I just really get fucked up. I don't have the kind of personality that can hold things in. For a lot of people in therapy, just talking fixes a lot.

It was a lot of work. I was probably nauseatingly into it for about six months. I think when you first start seeing a therapist, all you do is talk about it to everyone and bore the shit out of them. Of course, everybody is more interested in their own problems than in yours.

I don't see it as the kind of thing that has any stigma. I think maybe everybody at one time or another is in need of some perspective, and there was really no other way for me to get perspective at that point.

It was really coming to grips with what I was. Like it wasn't hip to be bisexual. Well, I was bisexual then. And I couldn't go around talking about it. No one around me could deal with it. I couldn't deal with it.

I decided to be myself, whatever the cost. This was in 1967, when you couldn't really comfortably discuss bisexuality. It's not something you comfortably discuss outside of major cities even now. But in 1967, no way: people were still getting married then, to "do what's right."

Artists are always supposed to be the gauge of what's happening. Camus said if you want to be a philosopher, write novels. If you want to be a philosopher now, you write songs. Someone like David Bowie is committed to living his life as it is, whatever the changes he's going through. And that includes just being straightforward when somebody asks you about sex.

I hadn't intended to mention that I was bisexual [during an earlier interview]. But the interviewer realized that I wouldn't lie. When I start lying, it becomes very pathological, and I just keep going. And I'm very uncomfortable with lying nowadays because I've been practicing telling the truth so long. So I didn't lie to this interviewer: I couldn't destroy my credibility with myself.

I always counted on my therapist through whatever I was feeling. I was really into being crazy at that point; I really enjoyed it. And he didn't make it pleasant either, which I think a lot of therapists do. He just didn't let up. He didn't say, "OK, you're crazy, I'm going to put you away for two months in a rest home." He said, "I'm sorry, but you've got to stay here and deal with it."

Even when I wasn't in the mood I always went, because I knew I had something to say. It was just a matter of saying it. Most artists—at least writers—tend to withdraw from things.

When they're getting crazy, they get numb. And I did the same. When you're numb, you really want someone to pull you out of it, but you can't; I mean, you won't let anybody in far enough to pull you out. I think when I couldn't talk it was more just being numb, not feeling—which is death for a writer. The worst thing for a writer is not to feel, not to be aware, not to let feelings in and out.

Right now I'm in the middle of a tour. I'll have one day about every two weeks where I'll withdraw mentally from everything. It's horrible; I hate it. It's not involuntary; it's just that if I don't do that, I'm going to get really weird. Better to withdraw mentally, because I can't withdraw physically; I'm spending all my time with fourteen other people. I think everybody needs space. It comes down to a territorial thing. You withdraw, you just don't talk to anybody for a day, you stay in your room—or when you're walking, you just walk and be quiet. But it's very difficult to get to a point where you can do that, *know* that you're doing it, and not be scared of it. I mean, I know that the next day I'll wake up and I won't be withdrawn. I know that my brain will have eased up and I will have had some time to just think. It's almost like meditation.

When I was sixteen I didn't know that, and I would withdraw for days. I would just hate everybody and get real depressed, and not talk and not eat. I was down to about seventy pounds. You can't bring somebody out of that until you can convince him that it's easier to come out of it than to stay there.

I was doing a lot of downs and stuff. The guy I was living with at the time, Peter, saved my life a couple of times. I withdrew because I needed to get some of that pressure off and talk to myself a little bit. If I had had the intelligence to go off to a retreat every week for a couple of months, I would have been fine. I just didn't give a fuck about anything, myself or my work—and when I don't care about my work, I know I'm really screwed up.

Being a writer is something you have to deal with. Dealing with whether you're going to drop everything and go write a song—say "Excuse me" and risk offending people—or whether you're going to be polite and sit there and lose the song. If you excuse yourself, people feel closed off from you, and there's no way to explain that to them except over a space of years. When I'm writing a song I tend to walk around the house completely *gone*. It builds up if you're living with someone: they get crazy. It's the same kind of numbness externally, except that you're really undergoing a lot inside. And it's very difficult for people around you to understand that if they're not writers—to understand how quickly it can go if you don't pay attention to it. Commitment is really what I got from therapy, a commitment to myself. I made a conscious choice. To be myself all the time, rather than never being myself.

I just mainly talked about what I was feeling and what I wanted to feel. I was getting in touch with anger, getting in touch with fears. I mean, I was never consciously scared as a kid: I was a heavy-duty, tough little broad. And I learned that it's OK to be vulnerable, it's OK to be scared. It hurts more initially, but then you find out there's really not that much to be scared of.

The kind of therapy I was involved in really made me see that everybody's human and everybody's got troubles, trite as it sounds. It's like what I said in "At Seventeen." Everybody's been held down for whatever reason. It's good to be able to admit to those things. I find that once I admit to something, it becomes less true and a lot less scary.

I think the biggest surprise of my life was finding out that everybody didn't love me. I mean, it was really a shock. And to discover that everybody, once they got to know me, wouldn't like me. I had thought, "They'll like me, sure, because I'm nice." I was twenty-two before I realized otherwise. It was a little late. It was after a very unhappy love affair, when I suddenly discovered that one of the people involved hadn't liked me—and still didn't.

I think that as an artist one is always scared that there's some deep, dark secret, that your work stems from the craziness. I think there's always the fear that your writing is coming from that place and the therapy is going to destroy it. I didn't find that; I found just the opposite. The more in touch with myself and the world I became, the less the non-writer I was, the more the words flowed.

It sounds like snobbism, but there is a difference between people I know who have been in any kind of therapy and the people who haven't—just in the way they relate to themselves. My generation are very concerned with their inner lives, as it were. My parents' generation were not, in the same sense, though they're having to be now. And the generation before them just didn't have time; they were too busy finding food. I think it was real good that I was in therapy at the age I was, because if I hadn't been in it, it would have been just that much harder later on.

In the end, all forms of therapy are basically getting you to help yourself. It's all Norman Vincent Peale in the end. What therapy really made me do was make me look at myself and help myself—with no pretense at anything else. You can't be let down then unless you let yourself down.

I think it's always a disappointment when you find out that someone is human and has his own hang-ups. This particular guy (my therapist) never returned phone calls unless it was an emergency. If he said he was going to give you a ring, he never did. Eventually I told him he was full of shit over this problem, which was just something that I felt should have been corrected. Stuff like that is a disappointment. You want people to be God. I think you are always looking for someone to be God. I know I am. All my friends are always looking for heroes. Anybody. But then what my own shrink did [not returning calls] was pretty minor. He never let me down—I hate to use the word "spiritually"—but he never let me down spiritually.

I was brought up with a very healthy attitude toward myself, which I think has probably seen me through a lot. I could be anything I wanted to be and I would be good at it. So far it's held up. It's a great thing to have been given by your parents. My parents encouraged me to *be*, which a lot of people don't receive. The idea of failure never existed for me as a kid. It never occurred to me that if I wanted to do something, I couldn't do it.

When I was twelve and fourteen it was really important to me to become a star and to be famous. Have millions of people clapping all the time. Now I really want to write. All this other stuff is transitory. Performing is nice, but it fades almost immediately after. You do a hundred and fifty shows a year, and it's fun, it gets your ego off, and it gives you a way of staying in touch. You can't afford to lose touch if you're a writer. If you lose touch, you die. So I sign autographs after every show, get to meet people, talk to them. I don't know what I'll do when I stop. I'll have to hire people to come and talk to me. And I have to stop touring sooner or later. It's pretty tiring. And it takes up a lot of time. I'll spend about seven months of this year on the road.

Back when I was younger, people were, in a sense, much more important to me than they are now. I would do almost anything to keep a friend. Now I'll do almost anything to keep a friend, but I know that, past a certain point, a person is no real friend. Years ago I would try very hard to act normal around my friends. And now—well, if I'm with a bunch of people in a restaurant and I get besieged for autographs, there's nothing I can do about it—except not to go to restaurants. Back then it would have made me crazy. I think I just accept things a lot more now.

I used to give huge amounts of money away. I pretty much gave away everything I earned to friends. I felt guilty at earning it when they didn't. I know better now. I know I work that much harder than anybody I know, and I deserve whatever I'm earning.

You always read in the fan magazines things like "Cher says 'I really think I'm ugly' " or "Carol Burnett says 'I always felt unloved' "—whatever. It's all a common denominator. The success you have—and I'm sure this is what drives a lot of older people who become stars into being crazy—doesn't really mean that much. In any kind of success, whether it's as a teacher or whatever. It doesn't fix anything; it doesn't change anything.

I think you have this magic goal, and if you accomplish it, you think it's going to change everything. Suddenly your skin will clear and you'll be incredible all the time: you'll become what you think all those people who are famous are. And it doesn't happen that way. But then again, you tell that to somebody and they're not going to believe it.

It's very hard to deal with something so removed from ordinary life as stardom. It's really not real. This room, for instance: there's a piano in this room! How many people walk into a hotel and have a piano and a refrigerator in their room? And this is nothing: this isn't even the world of rock 'n' roll.

I know that as a friend my therapist is there. He's a phone call away. I still see him whenever I'm in Philadelphia. I have dinner with him and his family. At this point we have a mutual respect for each other's work. I still have some unfinished business I should take care of with him—which I guess is what everybody always feels.

People tend to latch onto someone like me and tell me their life stories in three minutes. That's uncomfortable, because sometimes they start crying, and there you are, the receptacle; your shoulder is soaked and you can't help them. There's nothing you can do. I'm very uncomfortable when people try to get me to fix their lives, because I can't. They're asking for an answer and I don't have any answers. None. And if I did, I wouldn't tell them.

Nicholas Meyer

"I don't want to hold you up and I don't want to lead you on," said author Nicholas Meyer (*The Seven-Per-Cent Solution*), who was a month past deadline and more than a hundred pages away from completing his new novel. But ten days later he ushered me into his new house in L.A.'s Laurel Canyon for a chat.

Casual in a green-striped polo shirt, blue jeans and sneakers, he led me to his "cubby," which was identified as "The Dr. Watson Room" by a sign on the door. On the walls were mementos of the thirty-one-year-old Meyer's days as a movie publicist: the paperback cover of *The Love Story Story* (his behind-the-scenes account) and a picture of himself with Ali MacGraw. Reflecting his efforts as a novelist was an award from the Mystery Writers Association.

As we talked, Meyer sat behind his desk and puffed on a pipe not unlike Sherlock Holmes's (*The Seven-Per-Cent Solution* had the famous fictional detective teaming up with Sigmund Freud) while he expounded on his experiences with therapy.

Everybody decides to go into therapy for the same reason. Everybody goes into it because they are not happy. Either they are not happy with their work or they're not happy with their private life in some capacity or other. They can't sleep, they can't wake up, they cannot sustain a relationship. Their work is bothersome to them, or they don't perform it well. It's one form or another, and they're usually all interrelated. But people decide to get therapy when they figure out that their unhappiness, their failing—whatever you want to call it—is connected to personal difficulties which they may have shoved to one side for as long as they possibly could.

In my own case, I went into therapy in my junior year in high school. My mother had been ill for three years and had died of cancer. I was growing up in a house where this situation was hanging over me, and I was not very aware of what it was doing to me.

What I did know was that I was lonely at school, I didn't have any friends, I was not a successful student, nobody seemed to like me, and I didn't seem to like anybody. And, in addition, I had terrible headaches and stomach aches, the origin of which didn't seem to have anything to do with physical distress, because they were so arbitrary and consistent.

Part and parcel of this was an inability to express emotion of any kind, including crying. I hadn't cried when my mother died and didn't cry for some time thereafter. I seemed to get stomach aches instead.

I was desperately lonely throughout school, from the fourth grade on. I went first to a school called P.S. 183, a public school, and I loved it there—and had friends. Even so, I was already developing school problems. Then my parents put me into a private school, and from Day One at that school I was an outsider, and I remained an outsider, essentially, through the twelfth grade. There were a lot of things about the kids that I didn't respect to begin with. They were terribly bright, very spoiled, and as crazy as I was. They were very materially oriented, but, even so, I think I wanted desperately to be friends. The only people who were conceivably interested, though, were people who were at least as bad off emotionally as I or as ugly as sin. I knew I didn't want those groups; I wanted the smart, good-looking people with the screwed-up values. I saw a report card of mine once from the seventh grade that said I was aloof, cool. How strange that is when all I really wanted was to be in there with the other kids! I think that school did not judge me very well.

I was not doing well in school, and what was manifest to people who talked to me indicated that my grades did not seem to be commensurate with my intellect. People said, "You must be an A student." And I would smile wanly. I was a C student. One day my father suggested to me that maybe I could do with some help. And I said, "What does that mean, that I'm crazy?" He said, "If you were crazy, they'd come and lock you up; they'd take you away. Maybe you need some help."

My father, who is a psychoanalyst, recommended somebody, but the therapist was not a person who knew my father very well—or vice versa—so the connection was not suspect.

So for two years I went once or twice a week to see a psychiatrist in New York, and it was quite a remarkable and beneficial experience. It really turned me around from being a nonfunctioning person into somebody who was functioning to a considerable degree.

My big defense with people—and it was especially true in adolescence—was that I was a very entertaining fellow: a terrific story teller, a terrific joke teller. And since I had no idea what the process of therapy was supposed to be, I did one of two things. For six months I entertained the therapist. I just told him funny things and was cute and clever and beguiling. But there comes a time when you run out of that stuff—and he just waited me out.

The other thing I did was to use him to complain, as though he were an arbiter who was going to hear my side of my problems with my father. As though I were going to get judgment.

Sometimes I would be interrupted by his asking, "Have you ever dreamed? Do you have dreams?" And I would say, "Yes, I have dreams." I would tell him the dreams, and as I told him, they suddenly made a kind of shocking sense to me. I found myself blushing. I'd say to the doctor, "You have a terrifically filthy mind." And he'd say, "Wait a minute, wait a minute. Whose dream is it—yours or mine?" Occasionally he would make some suggestions to me based on what he heard. "Has it ever occurred to you that———?" With most of them it had never occurred to me that———. I'm sure I was a textbook case of repressed grief and a lot of other things.

When I was a little kid I tried to find out what my father did for a living. The best I could get out of it was that he was what I used to call a feelings doctor. My father said that was about the best description that he had ever had.

As I got older—this was unrelated to my therapy—I'd sit with him after dinner and he'd say to me, "What do you think about a person who does such-and-such?" "Sounds like he's afraid of so-and-so," I'd answer. "Yes, it does kind of sound like that," he'd say. And this is the way in which we would discuss patients. The result of this was *The Seven-Per-Cent Solution,* in which Sherlock Holmes meets Sigmund Freud, because it sounded so much like detective work. So much of it seemed to make common sense to me that a lot of the conclusions, anybody can come up with. It was asking the right questions, observing the right patterns. My father said, "I have a patient who always comes five minutes late. What does that sound like?" I said, "It sounds to me like he doesn't want to come, or he wants to show *you* that he doesn't want to come"—and so forth.

A lot of things that cropped up in my sessions with my psychiatrist were so astounding the first time out that I vehemently denied them. I'd say, "Oh, Doc, you're crazy; you've got one hell of an imagination." And then—perhaps even as I was denying it—my mind was inevitably turning over the possibility.

I once said, "Nothing here is really surprising me." And he said, "Nothing here will seem very new. It's only the connections that will seem new." So, in that sense, the results were extremely surprising.

The process is intellectual and requires a lot of concentration, a lot of seriousness. But you can't fool the doctor. There are people who play this perverse game. They think, "Well, I won't tell him what I really dreamed; I'll make up a dream." Which is always very funny, because you reveal yourself just as much in the dream you make up.

The experience of therapy is horrendous at times. The only question is whether it's more horrendous to go around walking into walls or to turn on the light. In fact, that was the image. I said, "Well, how's this process supposed to work?" He said, "It's very simple. Have you ever been in a room with the lights off?" And I said, "Yes. You bump into a lot of things, you trip over furniture, you walk into walls, and you knock down lamps—all things that would be absolutely absurd if you could see where you were going." He said, "Well, our job is to turn on lights so you can see these things and know how to avoid them or deal with them without being clumsy." There were times when lights were turned on that you wished they were turned off again for a while. It opened a bigger can of worms. But then it's a question of "Do you want to go back to bumping into lamps again?" And I had reached the point where I absolutely did not.

One reason was that I had an inner conviction that I was not an unhappy person, that I was a happy person, that I was just somehow missing the boat. I thought I was a person who was very gregarious, who ought to have friends, who ought to function a lot better. I shared the conviction of people who saw in me somebody who should get A's—but I knew that I wasn't. I thought, "I should get A's—why can't I study?"

There were parts of therapy that were extremely difficult—and you tend to blame the therapist at that point. You say, "It's all his fault. If I drop out of this, if I stop going, I won't have to sit there for an hour and waste my time doing this stuff." The therapist becomes like—well, you know what the Persians did to messengers who brought bad news. So you do away with the therapist. But this is specious; it doesn't stop the news.

More often than not, going to the sessions was something I wanted to do. One thing he never cured me of was my compulsiveness. I'm compulsive about doing what I say I'm going to do. I could see myself at a certain point dying in a car accident just to get someplace on time. And you ask yourself, "Why, why are you so afraid of being five minutes late? What do you think will happen? That they won't like you, that they won't be there?" Good questions. I was in such serious trouble in my life that this was the only thing I had going for me, so I don't think I missed very many sessions.

I was very lucky. I had no preconceived notions. When I grew older I heard a lot of people, particularly creative people, say, "Oh, I don't want to find out what makes me tick, because if I know what makes me tick, I won't tick anymore." The implicit assumption is made that one's creativity is directly correlatable to one's neurosis. Which is like saying, while you're sitting in a jet plane, "If I understood the physics that makes this thing fly, it would fall down." But there is no correlation. The physics makes it fly.

The funny thing about creativity in a lot of people is that, far from being a neurotic aspect of their behavior manifesting itself, it's probably the sanest thing about them. It's one of the oldest bugaboos that therapy will take it away.

What I expected it to do—and what I found it did—was to make me much better. Because I found there were certain things I couldn't tackle, be it studying or writing (which I was doing from the time I was five).

Writing is not what I want to do. At the moment, directing is what I want to do. Originally I wanted to be an actor, but I found out that I wasn't very good. And then I discovered directing. Then I started utilizing the writing as a way of getting to the directing. I've wanted to be a director for ten or twelve years. The writing has turned out to be a lucrative tangent and not an unrewarding one. But writing is just something I always do. Maybe I *am* a writer, but being a writer is something I didn't concentrate on wanting to be.

Anyway, if art is creative daydreaming/fantasy made conscious and organized, and if you look at several things you've done and discover certain patterns—like all the women are beautiful or all the women are ugly—not to be able to break out of those patterns is negative, if one wants to be the kind of artist I want to be. So what therapy did, I think, was enable me to branch out more. By striking down some of the mental roadblocks I had erected that were dictating a rather narrow, circumscribed area of fantasy life, therapy opened up my fantasy. I was now free to venture into uncharted waters.

I was in therapy in the middle of adolescence, and there were all sorts of questions about sex that you have to ask. Like "If you keep masturbating, will you use it all up?" My psychiatrist had a great answer for that one. He said, "Have you?" These questions about sex are ones you would ask anybody who would give you the information. In my case, it was my therapist.

Therapy is a field which, like show business, makes lots of space for mountebanks and charlatans and crazies. Out here [California], you know, therapy is very fashionable. People have live-in psychiatrists and psychiatrists who attend their parties. I just find it appalling; the whole idea of it seems to me really decadent. And you hear about psychiatrists marrying their patients. I used to think that was a totally venal thing—and certainly it is—professionally—totally wrong. But a psychiatrist friend of mine had a rather interesting explanation for it. He said that sometimes the patient is in so much trouble that the therapist finds himself marrying the patient in an attempt some way to supply what's missing.

The definition of a psychiatrist is a Jewish doctor who can't stand the sight of blood. Oh, I could tell you so many psychiatrist jokes. I mean, I grew up with psychiatrists. They had a poker game every month at our house. You haven't lived until you've seen a bunch of those guys trying to psych each other out over a poker table.

Certain ideas in therapy were quite novel to me. I'll give you one example that fascinated me. One day my father was moving books from the living room into the basement and I was helping him. We were listening to the phonograph while we were doing this. I had played three records which I had picked. At the end of the third record, my father put on a recording of Wagner, whom I despised at the time. I said, "I'm not going to help you move these books if we have to listen to that shit." And my father, quite rightly, was very annoyed. A big fight erupted.

I went to my therapist and told him all about the fight. The doctor said, "What books were you moving?" I told him they were some volumes in Russian that nobody but my mother could read. She wasn't there now, so we were putting them in the basement. And thereafter my therapist and I discovered—my father having remarried since—that whenever something of my mother's was moved to the basement, as had happened before, it was followed by a fight. It suddenly all linked up. I always managed to provoke my father in some way. Now, the advantage of this was that I came out of it knowing that the next time something of my mother's had to be moved out of the way—as reality dictated, for perfectly sound reasons—I should have a little bell go off inside me, watch myself, try to understand that I was upset by this, and deal with reality. My therapist was brilliant to ask me about these books. He might have said to me first, "Well, what were the three records you played?" That probably would not have yielded very much. But then again, he also happened to know that his patient had a mother who was recently deceased and his father had remarried. Still, it was a good question.

What makes a professional? It's not his clinical background. There's a wonderful line in *Richard II* that seems to be all about what this is about. Richard says, "Here have I the daintiness of ear." You have to hear really good. What you have to do is be very methodical. You sort out all the possibilities.

The major disappointment of therapy, it seems to me, is the slowness of it. All you can say is that you didn't get fucked up overnight and you're not going to get unfucked overnight.

There's no doubt that, in the larger sense, psychiatric therapy is a very limited tool. It only works for certain people, and there are certain things I think it probably doesn't do. I've asked my dad what it doesn't do. He said there are certain things like alcoholism that it doesn't seem to work very well with.

But it is largely used, in addition to its use with patients, as a research tool. As a research tool it's quite stunning. Psychoanalytic biography makes biography a twentieth-century art. Because the idea of not merely writing down the history of a man but also coming to some grips with interpreting that history—understanding motivation and so forth—is great. I mean, sometimes it has very literal application. You know about *The Mind of Adolf Hitler*? It uses the tools of the psychoanalyst and applies them to great effect.

There's a new book which is a psychoanalytic study of Nixon. And I think he's ripe for it, because he was so clearly a deeply disturbed person whose patterns were so obvious. Like his little slips of speech: "We must get rid of the farmer—I mean, we must get rid of the surplus" or "We can't stand pat" or "Just remember this: two rights don't make a wrong." I mean, this man was trying to tell you something. Think of his ordering the invasion of Cambodia two days after seeing the movie *Patton* for the second time. The whole thing with the tapes was a classic example. I mean, he convicted himself out of his own mouth and saw to it that it happened. It was as if he said, "Lest there be any doubt, here's my voice on the subject." I think he's fascinating material.

For psychoanalysis you have to have a lot of money, you have to have a lot of time, and you have to have a lot of patience. I think it's the impatience that generates all the other sort of short-cut things. LSD was the American answer—like everything else in this society—to the pushbutton concept. Pop a pill and get sudden insight. If you don't throw yourself out a window first, you've gone through eight years of analysis. That's *implicitly* the idea. I don't think there are any short cuts to human understanding. It takes a while, and any method of therapy that tells you "We can do it faster" is, in my opinion, full of bunk. I don't believe it.

During therapy I changed from a person who saw himself as a victim of inexplicable events and circumstances that he didn't seem to be able to control, to a person with a more realistic appraisal of what the true nature of my problems was—which is to say, what my own participation in them was. I recognized in a conscious way my own self-destructive tendencies, began to understand what those tendencies were and why they existed, and, as a consequence, became less self-destructive. I used to think about myself as a flop and a failure. Now I think of myself less and less that way. But it's still something I wrestle with.

The reason everybody is intrigued by success is that there is a myth that success will solve your problems, your personal problems. In fact, as far as I can see, there's very little correlation. On a very mundane level, if you think success will prevent your ever having to go to the bathroom again, you're wrong. You'll still have to go to the bathroom like everyone else. Take it from there and just extrapolate. In fact, success may throw your own personal problems into sharper relief, because suddenly you find yourself able to concentrate on them—and they're as big as ever.

What success does is gratify your ego in the broadest sense of the term—massage it—and pay your bills. That's the most immediate thing I can say about success. It bought this house; it enables me to make the payments on it. But I find that it has very little relation to how I feel about myself or my work. It's very nice to know that people loved *The Seven-Per-Cent Solution,* that they went crazy over it, but that doesn't really seem to impinge very seriously on my own estimation of that book's strengths and weaknesses—which may or may not be as accurate as the public's.

Somebody telling me that something I've done is great or terrible doesn't really affect in any lasting way how I see it. For instance, I think *The West End Horror* is a better mystery than *The Seven-Per-Cent Solution*. It was a successful book, but not as successful as *Seven-Per-Cent*. But for me it was a more important book. I felt that I grew with that book in terms of things I had learned how to do as a writer—and it made me happier.

When I get over hating my high school and am able to talk about it dispassionately, I'll consider it a major achievement. At the moment, talking about that place is like talking about yesterday, and seeing those people—and I have seen them—can throw me back almost into the same relation to them and to myself. It's very scary. I think it has a lot to do with things that were going on outside the high school that I sort of lumped onto the high school, like my mother's illness.

I strongly believe, by the way, in the therapeutic power of hatred. It keeps you alive, gets the blood going, gives you purpose. I find that real anger is a great stimulant. I'm the angriest person I know.

I'd like to be able to enjoy myself more, and I would like to become more flexible in the way I live. By "enjoy myself more" I mean I would like to have an even better opinion of myself than I have. Somewhere, when somebody points a finger at me and says, "You're guilty," there's still a thing in me that goes "How did he know?" not, "I'm not guilty."

I have a tendency in emotional situations to close off. I have this image of a ship with watertight compartments, and suddenly all these bells go off and doors want to close. And it's very unfair to the person I'm dealing with, because he doesn't know what's going on. I'm suddenly overpowered by the urge to read a book, to end the scene, not to play it out. I've learned as much from my girl friend as from my therapist. She's always explaining to me that it's better to let the feelings out.

One of my real ongoing problems is this self-knowledge thing. Frequently I'm not in touch with what's going on with myself. I'm a lot more in touch than I was, because previously I had *no* idea what the hell was going on. Now I have some idea, and I also have been given the wherewithal to find out the rest.

Susan Clark

Susan Clark attracted wide attention and acclaim for her television portrayals of golfer Babe Didrikson Zaharias in *Babe,* and America's best-known aviatrix in *Amelia Earhart.* Clark has also appeared in such films as *Maeigan, Coogan's Bluff, Tell Them Willie Boy Is Here, The Skin Game* and *Airport 1975.*

About six years ago I was in pain emotionally, and a very perceptive friend said he thought I'd feel a lot better if I went and spoke with a professional and kind of unloaded some of the pressure I was feeling. So he called his psychiatrist in New York and got a list with the names of four therapists out here.

One night I just broke down and started crying, and so I went in to see my GP. I mentioned the names of the psychiatrists who had been recommended to me, and he told me there were two who he thought might be particularly helpful.

I postponed calling anyone for about seven weeks. The excuse was that I was working, but that was just absolute bullshit. The truth was that I was scared to death. Nobody I knew well had been in therapy. And I think I had a lot of fears and hang-ups about it.

Finally I called up, and the man who answered the phone was a nice, responsible human being, not any sort of monster or someone who was judging me. He asked three questions: where I got his name, why I wanted to come, and how I was feeling. I told him, and he said to come see him the following week.

He was an older man, in semiretirement, but very good and very straightforward. I sat in a chair facing him for the first two or three months, and then, as we moved into another kind of more intense therapy, I was on the couch and he was behind me.

The therapy went on for about two years off and on. It would stop when I had to go out of town to a location and would resume when I returned. When I was in town I would often see him three days a week. The pressure—which is the only way I can describe it—started to go away after about the third month. I suddenly felt lighter.

When I came home from the sessions I would feel very tired, and frequently I would get into bed and sleep for an hour. I thought this was kind of strange, and it puzzled me for a while. But my psychiatrist said it meant I was working hard. He said that if a person went for any kind of analysis and came out feeling kind of happy and refreshed, he wasn't doing the work; he wasn't probing.

I think for a while my therapist was an authority figure to me. I would get a little cranky inside if I thought he wasn't listening. He would get very silent, look up and look away. After a while I realized he was thinking. And then I kind of tried to get into his head; I'd think, "My God, what must it be like sitting here for eight hours a day listening to all this garbage?" I used to enjoy it when I could make him laugh.

He would ask the same questions at different times, sometimes at the same session or sometimes over a period of months. And I used to think, "What's the matter with this guy? I already told him that—doesn't he remember?" But he was checking on me.

It wasn't difficult opening up to him in the beginning, because I had postponed it until this kind of pressure had built up inside. So, by the time I was there, boom, I just exploded like a pressure cooker. It all came out. My anxieties and poisons and God-knows-what had kind of bubbled up and out.

I think it's important for a person to wait until he's ready for therapy, until he's really receptive and willing to give and open up and do the work. Because any way you cut it, it's work. It isn't fun; it's frequently painful. And if you cheat or lie or evade, you're only cheating yourself.

One thing I feared before going into therapy was that the talent I possess, my creativity, would be exposed or damaged. I mean, that was a kind of nameless fear. Of course it doesn't happen if you have a good analyst. Your imaginative processes are simply cleared up; you get rid of a lot of the extraneous garbage that complicates things. You start to recognize the excuses for what they really are. I don't know that they actually change, but you can put them in a better perspective.

I was also terrified that the psychiatrist might be some kind of Svengali and that I might not be in control of things.

When I went into therapy, I wasn't in touch with my anger. I was really messed up about being a woman and being successful and ambitious and trying to keep a marriage together. One of the things I had been hit with when I arrived in Hollywood nine years ago was that I was "too intelligent," as if that meant I had four eyes or an extra breast. It was, "Hey, you're not going to get along here—you're too smart; you're smart-ass."

So I felt I was constantly in the process of hiding, although I didn't know what I was hiding. I would end up playing games. In business situations I thought I mustn't be aggressive; I must be charming. My instinct was to be quiet and, if I had an idea, to introduce it as if it were someone else's. Now I would say what I was thinking and not worry about what other people thought of me.

I used to hide a lot and put myself down. I know that I had great difficulty having fights with people and really telling it like it is. I would avoid ugly confrontations. It was like, "Don't make a scene. Scenes are unpleasant."

What other people thought was very important until I realized that deep inside me I couldn't give a shit, because it was me alone at three o'clock in the morning in the hour of the wolf. I had spent all this energy and time trying to please other people, but without any particular guidelines on how to do it.

Where I got messed up was in Hollywood. I mean the blocks and the defenses and the fears obviously had been there for many years, but they were being agitated by the system of being a piece of beef on a hook, which is what actors are in a big business situation. I was under contract to Universal Studios, and it took me a long time to understand the impersonal, computerized process by which they work. Therapy helped me put a perspective on all this.

In the beginning I think my therapy dealt somewhat with sex. I think after a while what happened was that we both realized that I really like men. Even though I was very much for the women's movement, I enjoyed men on all levels that I chose—as friends or lovers. I think I probably liked them more than women. Because when I was growing up, men were always more fun because they were going on to do things. The girls were talking about getting married and having babies, as if that were a profession as opposed to something that was a part of your life. So, to me, men were for a long time smarter, more fun and just better to be with than women, who were game playing.

I have had my share of being hurt and hurting, of being the "drop-er" and the "drop-ee," but I've never been abused or twisted in any way. I grew up totally accepted as a woman, and as a female actor in London from ages seventeen to twenty-two. When I came here at twenty-three, that's when the shit hit the fan. Men out here were impossible, just impossible. I mean, like the double standard, which I'd had no experience with. What I did was find other foreigners or other Easterners. They were not so much into that macho thing.

My therapist told me several things I've never forgotten, one of which was very applicable to me. He said it takes as much energy to listen as it does to talk. Nobody ever said this to me before, but it happens to be true. The concept is that usually people who talk are the ones who have all the energy and the people who listen are passive—but that's not true. Now, I knew this as an actress, but for some reason I wasn't using it in my life.

After the first year I realized that something inside my head and body recognized everything that was going down as being correct. It was like *déjà vu;* it was like I knew it, but I wouldn't recognize it—I wouldn't accept it. For some reason I was refusing to accept the responsibility of whatever it was, mostly me being a person. And that's something I didn't get from school, from home, from husband, from friends, anybody. Maybe I wouldn't allow it.

My fantasies and dreams were very full of anxieties and were painful, very tense. I had a recurring dream about the end of the world, which I'm sure was based a bit on *On the Beach.* I was a postwar baby and very much a child of the atomic age, so I am terrified of the bomb and the people who push the buttons. There's no such thing as a romantic war to me. Anyway, in my dream about the end of the world, there were bombs going off, and I was trying to escape to a place where I had been as a child, a fishing ranch in northern Canada. I used to have this dream off and on—I suppose that it was my own survival that I was confronting. But the therapist didn't want to spend a lot of time on dreams, mostly because my everyday life was so active and so full of ups and downs and contradictions.

After we had talked about my family for a while, I expected that wonderful deep, dark things would come out about my father, who died when I was young, when I was twenty. But the therapist said that that was not a problem area. "You had a very good relationship with your father—very healthy, very normal. He loved you very much and you loved him—and so I think we can leave that issue." I sort of thought, "Well, isn't everybody supposed to have a hang-up about his parents?" But I did have a better-than-average family background.

What I do think was important for me during my therapy was that I didn't stop living. I didn't treat myself like an invalid or like I had a serious problem so that I couldn't work. I carried on. I led a very normal life. And I had a lot of heavy decisions to make. Some relationships I found were very neurotic and others very positive. But I think it was the process that made *me* make those decisions, certainly not anything the psychiatrist said. He made no judgments.

The last time I saw him he cut the session short, which kind of surprised me, and said, "Well, that's it. You're a person now. Good luck." He said, "We've gone as far as we can go *at this point.*"

I think one of the things we disagreed about was something I couldn't articulate, which was women's roles and what should make a woman happiest. I think he was nudging me to make my own decisions on this.

I think if I were to go back into therapy again, I would seek a woman, a young woman. I don't mean a feminist, I don't mean a political woman; but I would find a woman. I just think that the problems I've had have been of identity and would be better investigated by another woman. I think she would understand faster where I was coming from.

If I went back now, it would be with other kinds of questions. There would be different areas I'd want to investigate. Is it possible to be all things? Is it possible to be a mother and have a career?

A female therapist would probably be in a similar kind of situation. She might have been married and she would understand that. She would have had to struggle in a very male-dominated world, the world of psychiatric medicine. She would probably be a few years older, but not that much; instead of being in her early thirties, she would be in her late thirties or forties. But there wouldn't be a big generation gap, as there was when I was in therapy before, when I was in my twenties and the psychiatrist was in his sixties.

There would be a lot of things I would like to talk to her about, including possibly sex and the nature of the orgasm. It's something a woman understands a hell of a lot better than a man; after all, he has a *male* orgasm.

I think the big thing is motherhood.

My marriage broke up about the time I was completing the therapy, but there wasn't any correlation. It would have ended anyway. I don't want to get married again, because I don't want to have to give up my identity and my name, and the laws require you to do that. It's hard for a man to imagine a lot of things, like how important it is to change your name. And vice versa, I'm sure, there are a lot of things men consider terribly important which women don't understand. For example, all of that concern over comparative penis length. A grown-up woman doesn't understand that. I mean, that's not how women choose men. We don't line six of them up and get out a ruler. And most of us don't like to be chosen that way.

At this point in my life I think I would go back into therapy as a healthy neurotic looking for more education, rather than out of desperate need. When I was most needful, I found a very good psychiatrist and got a lot of help from him, for which I'm very grateful. Now I would go on—as in a refresher course—and ask for other things. And the things I would ask for would be about women, because they would be about me.

Talia Shire

Not long after the Academy Award ceremonies at which she almost picked up an Oscar as "Best Actress" for *Rocky,* Talia Shire called to say the time for us to speak was at hand.

Before the statuettes were handed out, the twice-nominated actress was in a tailspin. Interviews and personal appearances, she told me, were robbing her of her creative energies and leaving her with nothing to say to anyone.

But now there was tranquility. As I approached her hilltop house in L.A.'s San Fernando Valley, only her dog's deceivingly ferocious barking disturbed the calm. Wearing a pin-striped shirt, jeans and sandals, Talia Shire was a fetching study, more relaxed and voluble than her public appearances had suggested.

While I settled on the couch in her library—dominated by a large framed movie poster from *The Lady from Shanghai* and a videotape setup—the petite actress slipped into a tiny chair that seemed designed only for a young child. Her admiration for her therapist—and her fascination with her role as a participant-observer in the therapy process—fueled an energetic discussion of her experiences.

About seven years ago, after my marriage, I was having a sleep problem. Essentially, I was going to sleep a lot. And this seemed peculiar to a friend of mine, who suggested I call up a clinic here in L.A. that has a bunch of good psychiatrists.

My family is very wary of psychiatrists. I think the hardest thing I had to fight constantly was my family's notions of what the therapy situation was, their paranoia. I was the baby in the family, and actually, even though I'm only seven years younger than my brother Francis [Ford Coppola], I'm like generations younger.

I find the process of therapy fascinating. And indeed, when you are an actress, you are like a psychiatrist with your characters—you explore them.

Now, I loathe traditional Freudian therapy or people who are in therapy for twenty zillion years and need to go there five times a week. Some therapists and some people do want a relationship that goes on for all their lives. That's a different kind of therapy. It's not even analysis. You know what it is? It's one of two things. Sometimes you don't have anything to do—there's a lot of boredom happening, and you need to get up. So a few times a week you know you have to get up at nine o'clock in order to get to the therapist at ten—and your day gets shaped. For others, who are not married or don't have good relationships, the therapy situation is like a marriage.

Anyway, I wanted another kind of therapy, and I got it. It was more eclectic; it was based more on a kind of love relationship between the two of us, and it was very fast. I was there about once a week for two and a half years. In and out. And he's still my dear friend.

My therapist was a terrific doctor named Robert Hinshaw. Originally I went to him wanting him to make me a good wife, make me efficient, make me an executive in my house. I had just gotten married, and I had no idea how to run a house.

But he didn't work on making me a good wife. He did a wonderful thing. He tricked me. Instead of our talking about it, he would play tapes of scenes from plays that dealt with marriage, using plays and actors that I respected, like T. S. Eliot's

The Cocktail Party. He sort of did what Rollo May does, a very creative thing. So what he did was make me love acting all over again.

I told him I couldn't act because I had terrible stage fright. He said, "Well, I'll go with you to an audition." He said, "If you were afraid of airplanes, would you want to spend ten years figuring out why, or would you want to go up for a fifteen-minute flight and then work your way up to being able to spend longer in the air?" And then he said, "Do you want to spend ten years trying to figure out your stage fright, or go audition for some crummy thing and get it over with?" I thought it was such a kind thing for him to offer to come along to an audition that I went to one without him. I went to audition for some little thing in the San Fernando Valley—I *did* it. That was my first triumph.

I went into my therapist's office with a bottle of champagne when I got the Academy Award nomination, and we laughed, because in a way he was part of that. His thing for me was action.

I was making changes in my life and I was getting a little scared. Part of my dilemma was that I was afraid of taking action, because every time I did, things happened. The way I was brought up it was difficult for me to understand that if I was bold, had my own identity and took action, it didn't necessarily mean that I wouldn't also enjoy a happy marriage and being a mother. Or that the men in my family would abandon me or not love me.

In fact, the message that I had gotten as a child—even though it was *not* given to me by my parents—was that if you compete and do really well, you're being unfaithful to something—whatever it was. It came a lot from the times. Girls were there to marry great men. You know what the myth is, that the woman is the muse. My mother seemed to devote herself to my father. So I picked it up.

I was constantly sabotaging myself. I was a very creative person who just spent the so-called golden years of high school—when you're supposed to be active—looking totally inactive. I was very deeply involved in this inner thing that was happening, which Dr. Hinshaw was the only one (later) to see as terrific.

I told him I used to break everything down to male and female. I used to enjoy setting the table because I had it all down to masculine and feminine. I very often would set that table in the form of a drama. The salt was always female, the pepper was always male, and the salt was always half full. I never would permit the salt ever to look full like the pepper. And I realized why: the females in this drama were always stronger than the males, and I never wanted men to look bad.

I guess I picked up something also that my brother told me, which was that men are very, very vulnerable—more vulnerable than women. He said you must be kind to them, never hurt them. If they need a lot of ego stuff, he said, it's because they're not nearly as strong. He told me one day always to be nice to boys, because they can be destroyed by a woman much more than a woman could ever be destroyed by a man.

There was a recent study that showed that when a man finally falls in love and the relationship doesn't work out, he can't recover as quickly as the woman. You men are very sensitive beings. I always had a tremendous sense of this with me, and I was constantly sabotaging myself. Never, never would I make a man feel that he was ever going to be hurt or in jeopardy or that I would ever want to outdo him.

I was really very well loved in my family, deeply loved. I had the golden childhood from one to five, and apparently that is a critical period, as it's when you're given your world view. I wanted to be sick and crippled, because that would have relieved me: I wouldn't have had to do anything. But I discovered that I had been given a lot of love and was healthy, and there was no way I was going to get out of being a person who would have to take responsibilities.

It took the therapy for me to realize that the bizarre way I had rerouted my energy—by sleeping—wasn't working, and that it was also a big lie for me not to compete with anyone in my family, which is what it was all about.

I did a classic thing when I got married. My father was a composer. I thought he was a great man who was not getting a break, and that it would be wrong for me to be happy and do well in school. Since I was deeply involved with my father, I was in the midst of a great tragedy, as I saw it, when I was a young girl.

And I realized early in my marriage what I had done. I had re-created literally all the obstacles of my adolescent years. I had married a composer, a very sensitive and complicated man with similar obsessions to my father, a similar life-style, similar work habits, and similar energy in the way he claims space. And I was either going to lose my identity again or I was going to get it this time. The therapist helped me do the latter.

I think I changed my role in that I decided not to be a wife so concerned with whether the dinner party worked or not, whether I made it to a January white sale, or whether my home was decorated.

I think I had taken a bum rap in my family a bit too much because I kind of had a meandering period. I think they wondered what I was doing. I couldn't quite fall into the role, on the one hand, of the sweet thing who married at twenty-two. And I couldn't quite execute my creative thing, because I didn't want to be in competition with my brothers, which would not have been in my nature. And I think it looked real peculiar to my family. In therapy I found out I was probably one of the healthier members. My position in the family was as observer. I watched them operate, knew how they were motivated, knew what they did, and was just real tuned in to them.

The reason I was always sleeping right after I got married, of course, was that basically I didn't want to deal with my particular dream as an actress. I wanted everything cut off. And my stage fright was all part of that fatigue thing.

I am told that I got myself a rare and different kind of therapist because he knew that I had spent most of my life with thinking and [self-] analysis and I desperately needed action. I was fortunate in finding him.

To me it was a privilege to see this man, to have my own professor, my own Aristotle. I never abused it. I didn't fuck around, in other words. I listened to everything he said. I could tell you what went on in the first meeting. So I would listen and I would change. Apparently I was a very good patient because I really wanted to transform myself and convert negative things into positive things.

I would come in with a week's notes I had on the relationships happening around me. And I trusted him. He traded me secrets, too. I would *never* tell a therapist anything if he didn't tell me something about himself. Because I am experiencing that man on many energy levels, as he is doing with me.

Mostly it's a very interesting exchange that's taking place. But I suspect this man could have been reading the telephone book and I would have been somewhat transformed. He was taking me in and converting something by basically his own energy and the fact that he was a loving, lovely gentleman.

He said that when he first started out, he was one of those therapists who didn't say too much. And now, obviously, he was a man fighting me for time to talk. I had expected a man who was going to sit back and do nothing—and that I was going to lie down. He told me, "If you lie down, you'll probably fall asleep." Freud used the lying position because he had a phobia about seeing people.

A lot of doctors will tell you you're sick and you will conform to that. You're putty in their hands. All my doctor was doing was reaffirming the fact that really I was a strong human being.

I think another thing that hooked me up with the doctor was that he had a lot of missionary zeal and basically I was very messianic. And when he could reconnect me with that in terms of my work, make me think that perhaps I could heal and change people, he hooked me up to that kind of messianic thing.

After my baby was born, about eighteen months ago, I was real depressed. He had a tremendous infection, and when I brought him home they told me there was a good chance he'd have palsy. It didn't happen. They also thought he might be deaf. He was not deaf either, but it took six months to find that out. It was really a grueling year in which I had to reexamine a lot of things about myself.

I realized I'm not good at self-protection. If somebody were to smack me or beat me up or mug me, I'd probably invite him to the house and say, "Listen, live here for a week." It's because I have to work from compassion.

During my depression I went to my therapist again one time. I told him, "I feel like I've fallen from grace. I have not an imaginative thing in my mind." It was a loss of access to my creative energies. But not really. Basically it passes. But it took one fucking year to do. I told my husband, "This has been one of the major depressions of my life," and he said, "I really didn't notice." We go through these cycles—God knows what does it—but they're incredibly creative times if you have the courage to ride them out. I was doing *Rocky* during this period, and it was agony for me to go to work.

My doctor has always said that I am one of the few people he knows with both feet firmly planted on the ground of reality and who is also totally eccentric and from Mars in my head. That's also a tribute to his therapy. He didn't want to take away my eccentricity. You know, artists are afraid of that. I'm really quite a crazed person—who's very in touch with the intuitive part of myself—and he never took that away.

I'm not by nature a whiner or a complainer. I'm a hysteric. That's what he told me. I'm not a depressive and I'm not a schizophrenic, which are a couple of good things not to be. I get disillusioned, but basically I'm not nervous-breakdown material.

I guess my point of view is that we're all victims here. I have this philosophical thing—I've always had it—that life is rough. And in my upbringing I never expected to be the queen of the world, ever. I think a lot of people who go into therapy go into it because they thought everything was orbiting around them, and therefore they're a victim. And I just automatically can tell you, of course, you're a victim; you're on this planet. Life is very hard. It's based on releasing. You've got something nice, you're going to have to give it back. And that's all there is to it. You might as well roll up your sleeves and get to work. You tell me something is an obstacle, I tell you I will make it into an opportunity for growth and character-building.